Santa
and the
Candy Cane Heart

John 3:16 - For God so loved the world that He gave His only begotten Son, that whoever believes in Him should not perish but have eternal life.

Santa

and the

Candy Cane Heart

Real Stories from a Real Santa

John Campbell

This book is dedicated with thanks to our

Lord Jesus Christ
who plans my schedule, inspires my
heart and blesses my hugs in His name

I want to acknowledge the support and
dedication of the following special people:

my wife, Ellen
my daughter, Stefanie
my grandson, Johnathan
my son, Sean
our parents and extended family
special friends and all the others
who have supported this ministry for 37 years

Table of Contents

Philippians 2:8-11 - And being found in human form, He humbled Himself by becoming obedient to the point of death, even death on a cross. Therefore God has highly exalted Him and bestowed on him the name that is above every name, so that at the name of Jesus , every knee should bow, in heaven and on earth and under the earth. And every tongue confess that Jesus Christ is Lord, to the glory of God the Father.

John Campbell

How This Santa Began

"I hear something rustling back in the sacristy! Will someone come up here to help me investigate? I am not certain I want to go by myself." Soon the door to the sacristy opened and two little children with mouths and eyes wide open stood looking up at me. They were stunned. The priest took my hand and led me out in front of the altar. There was applause and squealing and laughing in the packed church. When we got to the lectern he turned to me and said, "Santa, these children are hoping you will be coming back later tonight with something for them. Do you have a message for them now?"

Can it be 36 years since Father Carlozzi first asked me if I would be the Santa Claus at the children's service on Christmas Eve? Frankly I was skeptical that such a stodgy Episcopal parish as ours would stand for such a dramatic change in their afternoon service where children dressed in their finest velveteen outfits and come with parents and grandparents to sing carols and present gifts for baby Jesus. Santa was simply not part of the program.

Father Carlozzi had recently come to All Saints Parish in Phoenix, Arizona following the death of the founding rector. He explained that in his earlier parishes it helped young children unify the stories of Christmas if Santa came to church to tell them stories about Jesus' birth being the reason for the toys.

"You see", he said, "Each of the children comes to church knowing the toys will be coming later that night. They have been properly taught about Jesus' birthday, too, but the toys...that is what is on their minds."

When I agreed to be the new Santa, he told me, "Rent the best suit you can find. We don't want any scroungy looking Santa here. After all, you will be explaining Jesus coming to earth to these little ones. You have to look the part!"

I found a suit. I ordered candy canes. I prepared a small story and prepared to wait for the end of the service. The door had opened. We had left the children wide eyed and gone to the lectern. It was my chance to speak to the children of all ages gathered that Christmas Eve about Jesus and why we celebrate His birthday.

 Without hesitation, I told the children, "I will come back tonight when you are sleeping, but I wanted to take a few minutes now, in church, to remind you why I will be bringing you gifts later. You see Jesus came many years ago to live on earth. He gave us the greatest gift of all--His love and the forgiving of our sins. Because of that great gift, we all like to give gifts to remind our family and friends that we love them and that God loves them!"

With that Father Carlozzi signaled for the final hymn and taking my arm, headed me down the aisle during the recessional.

The going was a little slow for both of us. He was wearing a long damask cope and alb. I was wearing a red corduroy suit and a thin rented beard. The children and adults wanted to shake our hands, to hold onto our legs.

Finally we made our way to the patio outside where boxes of candy canes were waiting. That first year, we did not anticipate the mob scene around Santa. Soon family volunteers came to help open boxes and hold up the canes for Santa. Nearly 500 canes were given out in about 5 minutes.

Only then did the families look out to see that dusk had come and they could see the hundreds of lighted luminarias lining the walkways and patios of the church. "Oooh" could be heard moving down the line of moving people.

In the tradition of the Southwest, it was time to light the way of the Christ Child at the time of the celebration of His birth.

How Does Santa Look?

How do I get involved in some of these affairs? What is a guy from a blue-collar family home in the south doing in some of the fanciest homes in the country? How do I find myself by beds in a hospice or holding a lady over 100 years old on my lap?

Because I am Santa. I am a symbol of love, unprejudiced and universal.

People have a perception of how Santa Claus should look. He should be tall. He should be a bit round. He should look GRAND. The fur should be real. The boots shiny leather. The bag BIG and stuffed full of secrets. He should be someone who can be trusted. There should be a "Presence".

This Santa is six feet two inches tall, heavy enough not to need pillows, and has blue eyes that are memorable to those who see me. I have always tried to uphold the words of one reporter who stated in an article about me, "His bright blue eyes, rosy complexion, and robust build make him what many have called 'the perfect Santa."

For several years I added items to the costumes I have worn. Nature soon demanded I add a pair of glasses to insure I could read the maps to homes or the children's notes of wishes and love.

I made sure they were gold rimmed and look like the ones in the picture made popular by the folks at Coke. I ordered shiny black patent leather and found a shoemaker who would cover my belt and boots with it.

Often I encounter blind people. When they have friends or other assistance, they know Santa is there. I always stop to talk to them and encourage them to "look at me" with their hands. They especially enjoy the feel of the velvet and the white fur. The blind inspired the next addition to my costume.

We used Indian dance bells and laced them into white fur to put around my ankles. The bells are part of the mystique this Santa brings with him. Many wonderful experiences have been prefaced with the words, "I thought I heard bells. I had to see who had the bells." Now even blind people know I am on my way.

"I thought it was going to be you." The woman was leaning over a railing 5 floors above the atrium where I was standing asking me to look up for her to take my picture. People come from elevators, doorways, cafeterias, their own office parties. They reach out and wave, they whoop and holler to get my attention. I try to acknowledge everyone, but many people want to take me to their own corner of the world. I go when I can, but often I am on my way to an event with a time schedule and cannot accommodate everyone.

Through the years I have worn out 10 velvet suits and 6 beard and wig sets. You see I wear the suit from the first thing in the morning until I go to bed at night from December 1 through late on Christmas Eve. It is usually warm in Phoenix in December and it is always warm inside when numbers of children are crowded eagerly around me hoping to touch me or to receive a gift. When one's head and face are covered by the beard and wig, there is not much skin left for breathing and heat release. If I am fortunate enough to come home for dinner, I always leave wearing a fresh wig and beard (read "dry") and often a new costume coat.

The newest wigs are made of yak hair...a course natural hair. I have had hairdressers work on the wigs and beards just before Christmas Eve service and at the end of the season. It was funny for me to see my beard in curlers sitting under a hair dryer in a beauty shop. The image people have of what Santa should be is important.

Children are direct. Frequently one will state seriously, "Your beard is fake. I can see the string going up into your hair. You can't be real if your beard is fake." I try to have an answer for anything, but it is difficult to keep ahead of children. Now I take their hand and gently place it up under the long costume beard. Their eyes open wide in amazement when they feel my own real beard underneath!

I say, "You know people believe Santa should have a beautiful long white beard like this one. They would not like to see it full of paint and glue from making the toys all year. So I keep my own beard cut short to keep it out of the paint, but at Christmas I get out this long curly one so that people will be happy with how my beard looks." The child nods seriously and knowingly and goes off to tell anyone who will listen the revelation they have received.

Since 1999, when nature made my natural beard white, I have not needed to wear the artificial whiskers. I let it grow for 5 months to attain the length people associate with a "proper" beard for Santa. It curls and waves nicely.

I look at the fanciest Santa Claus at the Macy's parade and places like that to evaluate my costume. They are wearing gloves! I was given a nice pair of white gloves. I put them on and then I realized that I could not wear them as part of my costume. The Santa I convey, the love I bring to people could not be brought through the gloves.

It is my touch--the personal touch--hand on hand or hand on brow that conveys my love and God's love to the people who want to see Santa. Some of the hands are dirty, some are bloody, others have AIDS or cancer or sores, but I want to touch them directly so they will know they are loved.

Familiar, But Special

The young girl lying pale in the hospital bed looked as sad as anyone I believe I had ever seen. Her father had told me she had had a surgery to remove a cancer. She was healing, but she seemed so depressed that he wondered if she could possibly get well. He was tired from the stress of having her ill and caring for her young children, but his spirit was weighed down more by the thought that she would not try to recover.

It was December and I was wearing the red Santa Claus suit. Usually people hear the bells on my boots as I walk down hallways and are waiting for me to appear, but this girl didn't seem to realize I was there. I took a deep breath, breathed a prayer, and walked around her bed to face her with smiling eyes and a gentle, "Merry Christmas". She roused a bit and smiled at me, calling me by name.

"Thank you for coming", she said. I guess my Dad asked you to come."

"No, actually I decided to come myself. You see there was something making such a fuss in my red bag out in the car, that I could hardly think about driving. I stopped and looked inside and look at what I found".

I brought a small stuffed koala bear out from behind my back and gave it to her.
"Oh", she beamed. "Is this for me?"

"Just for you, from Santa", I said.

The miracle worked. The free gift. What made it so surprising this time is that this girl had held literally thousands of identical koala bears before.

I had met her when I first started visiting nursing homes as Santa Claus. I had learned that stuffed animals make such a difference to anyone who is sick, lonely, old, hurt, or afraid. And a stuffed animal from Santa Claus! It can make an entire year or lifetime happy. Finding enough affordable stuffed animals for each one I saw became a problem.

After several false starts, I had been referred to this young girl's dad. He sometimes sold his uniquely designed animals that were less than perfect for his use. He sold them to me in quantities I could afford to pay from my own funds for several years. Each December I would go to his business and select as many as I could afford and then he and his family would toss in more for "needy children".

So she had known me for several years. She had even seen me as Santa. I always tried to drop in on them in my costume to deliver a candy cane, have a picture taken with them on my knee, and thank them for making this special ministry with the animals possible.

"The animal must not be the miracle", I realized. It was the tangible item that conveyed the love with which it was given. I represented God's love, visiting her and loving her and giving her a gift....one of her own bears.

She was beaming when I left and her father told me that day was a turning point in her recovery and in her life. Her children got back their mom. Her family was restored their daughter. She was back at work soon and stayed well. She was still smiling years later.

For 12 years her father made sure I had all the animals I could give away...at greatly reduced prices...even by the trailer load sometimes. He would call up and say that he had found quite a few "rejected bears" that were sometimes raccoons or elephants.

He always thought of me, Santa, because of the miracles those little animals wrought. He once said, "I couldn't really believe the stories you would tell me about how you gave those bears to give hope and joy to people, until I walked into my daughter's hospital room and saw her smile as she hugged one of those tiny koala bears from my storage bin."

YES, VIRGINIA, SANTA IS REAL AND HE IS FREE!
The Stroller

Often thoughts of Santa Claus bring memories of snow covered roofs, icy roads, and clouds of mist growing with each breath you take as you traverse slippery sidewalks in boots and gloves. But for many children of all ages Santa comes in rainforests and in deserts, too.

Imagine being Santa in 85-degree temperatures with no relief from the heat of wearing wig, hat and costume for hours. Santa is a popular guest at party after party, nursing homes and church services. On many December days I get up, brush my teeth and don the Santa costume for the entire day. It is not possible to eat in the costume. I don't mind spending the day a little hungry, but I live in the desert and I drink a lot!

One night nearing Christmas, I had run out of bottled water in my car, so I stopped at a drive-thru restaurant for a cup of ice and a beverage. While I waited to be served, I carefully placed a Turkish towel into my collar and arranged it over my velvet jacket, white fur and velvet pants. Several years before I had learned that a drop of liquid mashes the velvet, forever. I looked up and paid the young clerk at the window with dollars and a candy cane. Her friends came to shyly ask for a candy, too. The more I smiled, the bolder they became..."Why are you wearing a bib?" asked one.

I was about to answer her when something moving in front of the car caught my eye. I saw a shivering girl with a rickety stroller looking at me with disbelief or fear.

I waved goodbye to the giggling window clerks and pulled slowly forward until I could see the young girl's face. She looked down, too. Thinking she was wondering why I wore the bib, I was about to answer the question, when I realized she was looking at a baby about 4 months old wearing a very dirty blanket. Kicking her thin blanket as she gurgled, the baby didn't notice her poverty or her mother's fear.

I reached into the other seat beside me and got several candy canes and handed them to the young mother. She reached out her hand to take them, but then she saw that I was also offering a big white teddy bear with a yellow bow. Slowly she pulled back her hand and shaking her head slowly, she asked, "How much is it?"

"Like Christ's love for us all, it is free" I said. "Someone who has gone before has paid for it to remind you that you are loved...no matter what. Please keep the bear and tell your little girl that Santa made a special gift to her so that she would always remember Jesus came at Christmas to show her God's love."

Recognizing relief and some relaxation in the young mother's face, I remembered Mary who had to endure much being the mother of Jesus. I drove away with a reverent heart.

The Real Santa

I was surely turned around and lost that Sunday afternoon. I knew I would not find the elderly priest I sought in the hospital maternity ward, but here I was and swamped with little children. Until you have worn a long fluffy wig and beard, you cannot imagine how little peripheral vision is left. I was afraid of stepping on one of the tiny children who grabbed me at every angle.

My own grown daughter was with me and quietly said, "Santa, this tiny one behind you wants to say something." That was my cue to stoop and reach behind to pick up the one clutching the back of my boots. I was learning. It was my second year being Santa. Father Carlozzi had told me to buy the best suit they make this year to be Santa. I did and began to wear it as soon as I could.

I visited the church folks who were sick. I stopped at parties at homes I saw just driving by. Everyone loved having Santa at their party and there are many people today who still wonder who that Santa was who came one year.

I enjoyed being Santa. I loved the way it feels to make people happy. I really enjoyed the opportunity being Santa gives me to touch people's hearts.

But I was in the hospital to find the sick priest.

My daughter had gotten directions to his room and we were about to leave maternity headed in the right direction when I noticed a little girl about 4 years old standing across the room frowning at me. I got down on my knee and called to her to come to see Santa. She just shook her head.

"You're not the real Santa" she shouted. The other children looked surprised, but not disappointed. They knew. They had had their hug and candy.

"Oh, come and feel his fur" encouraged my daughter, "then you will know that he must be the real Santa". "This is really soft velvet and fur."

She came slowly over, rubbed the fur, smiled a bit, but remaining unconvinced.

My daughter leaned over to her and asked, "Now that you've seen him up close, don't you think this Santa must be real?"

The little girl crossed her arms, took an adult posture with legs apart and stated at the top of her voice, "No. My mommy said the REAL Santa is at Chris Town Shopping Mall!"

Trust

Did you know it is impossible to have fun until you can relax and let yourself find enjoyment? To relax, you must first find an element of trust for where you are even if that is the tallest roller coaster. My grandchild enjoys the thrills and the speed of any ride; my daughter enjoys watching his pleasure but is hesitant about the ride itself; my wife screams in fear and swears she will never go again. She has no pleasure because she has no trust...except in Disneyland. Walt Disney convinced us that no one gets hurt there. It is a "Magic Kingdom".

A merry smile under the false white beard makes my eyes twinkle and bright. The red suit and jingly bells on my shiny boots complete the image of one of the most trusted symbols of joy in America...Santa Claus. People of all ages smile back at me, raise their arms to hug me, or run joyously up to hug my knees. At least that response is the one most common for me.

During each childhood there is one year when there is only mistrust. Mommy and Daddy are comfortable protectors and the child will not let go of their parent. I try the lure of candy cane held stretched out.

sually it is refused. I try coaxing them to look into the magic red velvet bag, but they shake their head, "No".

As the years have gone by I have learned that families still want pictures of their child with Santa, however, so I persuade the parent to come to sit on my lap...but that means they have to bring the distrusting child along...and so the picture can be made without any trauma to the little one.

I learned to ask a little one who will walk up to me, but will not sit on my lap, "Will you show me the back of your shirt?" That posture presents their face for the camera with Santa in the background and makes a nice picture for the album.

Beautiful black eyes filled with tears fill my memory of one little beauty. She was about 3 years old when she was adopted from Thailand by loving Phoenix parents. She was gracefully learning so much about our customs that were so new for her. Instead of taking her to a shopping mall, her parents thought a personal home visit with Santa the first year would be quite special. Her grandparents and other family were there when I arrived.

It was not surprising to me that she did not immediately run to me for a hug and candy. After all, I was very big....and very noisy...and very red.

Her grandparents, her parents, their friends all became embarrassed, however, when her shyness stretched beyond a few minutes. Still I was not surprised. Eventually I sat in a chair in the corner and just stayed still while the party went on without us.

Occasionally she would glance my way and more tears would pour down her cheeks. She knew that her family had expectations of her and those expectations concerned ME.

After an hour had passed and everyone was successfully ignoring me, she began to move closer. The candy had not left her mind. Soon she was reaching for the cane lying on the floor just out of my reach. Warily she crept up to it, her eyes never leaving mine as if daring me to reach out for her. Once the candy was successfully snagged, she stood to eat it.

Before many more minutes, she had begun to trust that I would not grab her or take her against her wishes. At that point she agreed to sit on my lap for pictures.

Her parents and grandparents never forgot that night. We all learned a lot about patience and trust. That little girl still gives me hugs when we meet, even when I am wearing the red suit.

Santa Transcends Time

From the very old who remember Santa from childhood days and love to tell him about their early toys, to the very young whose parents want to have their picture in his arms to show them how loved they were from the very beginning, Santa is a part of life.

I had been inside the hospital just at the ending of visiting hours to see a lady from our church who was dying. We had a nice visit, shared a prayer and a hug, and I was leaving to go home. This was a time when my heart was a little heavy from being tired, from watching my friend suffering, and from saying a final "goodbye" to her. But Santa must be Santa all the time, so I was walking with my head up taking care to walk slowly to keep soft the volume of the jingling bells on my boots, but smiling and waving when I saw someone wave to me in a hallway.

I had made it across the lobby and had just activated the automatic exit doors when a very excited young man came through them and said, "Wait right here...please wait right here."

Only then did I notice a car pulled up to the curb with its doors open. The young man had grabbed a wheelchair marked "admitting" and raced back through the doorway.

 He was being quite gentle and careful with helping a woman out of the car and into the wheelchair. Slowly, he pushed her through the open doors and up to me.

The bundle in the lady's lap moved and I could finally see that it was a baby! The young father asked me if I would wait for his brother who had a camera because they wanted a picture of the baby with Santa. He was 3 hours old.

My heart swelled with joy. What an exciting way to end a day with the very earliest beginnings of life in my arms! By the time I had thought of a place to stand away from the drafty door for the picture, 10 more people came bursting through the door and one was waving a camera high in the air! Two carloads of family had come to bring this mother and home delivered baby to the hospital to be checked over.

We took pictures. Family was there. Nurses were included. Santa and the baby were in every picture.

From encountering someone in the last hours of life on earth to someone who is having his very first hours here, there is blessing in all our God given LIFE.

Someone to Love Me

The massive assembly room was filled with presents and party food. There were recorded Christmas carols playing...too loudly it seemed because there was almost no other sound. "What a strange crowd," I thought. Usually when Santa makes an entrance there are pleasant sounds of welcome, applause, squeals of delight. But not here.

Instead I looked out at 50 pairs of eyes which followed me as I circumvented their chairs to go to the front of the room. I usually hand out many candy canes to the outstretched hands as I go by crowds to the front. Here there were no outstretched hands.

I arrived at the front of the room with all of my candy canes. I found the chair for Santa and turned to smile at the people gathered. Even though most of them were children, they had not crowded around me touching and listing their wishes.

The adult volunteers were doing their best to make a festive occasion. "Oh, look. Santa is here." "Hi, Santa...I've been good. Do you have a gift for me?" they said with excited voices as they looked hopefully at the young ones near them. The only response we could see was their unwavering eyes trained on me wherever I moved.

These children were all in the county detention system. Their parents were in jail.

Most had been abused during their short years in some, if not many, ways. I had thought I was prepared, but what I saw in their eyes was pain beyond most adult experiences. I wondered, but was not sure I wanted to know their stories.

Quickly the volunteers organized the kids into lines to greet Santa. There were bags of gifts supplied by organizations. I had my stuffed animals and candy canes. Curiosity got most of the children on their feet in the line. They couldn't tell exactly what gifts were in the bags.

Hoping for certain items, they inched forward and sat on my lap...even the big boys after a little coaxing and joking. They left my lap with a little relief in their eyes and sometimes a smile. Gradually the room atmosphere lifted and they began to eat the food and joke a little with someone or with me.

The last ones in line were eager to come. Something good was happening there besides the bag of gifts. I was able to transfer some sense of worth to each one letting them know I loved them. It was a bigger job than bringing a sack of toys. It had to be enough to last them for a long time...until they could get into normal life somewhere.

Finally I thought everyone had come to see me, but there were several bags left by my chair. I looked around and then I saw her. She was chubby, not very pretty, awkward by her uneven growing, and looked about 13 years old.

She stood as far from me as she could get in that huge room. She stood tightly against a wall, yet hunched like an old woman. Her sweater was stretched, her pants were a little short, but it was her demeanor that made her look abandoned.

I called to her encouraging her to come to see me. "You may be the last, but I have something wonderful for you," I said. She made no move. She just stared. Volunteers had been alerted, however, and two went to escort her to Santa. She walked between them, obediently, reluctantly.

When she got up to me, I offered my knee for her to sit as the others had. She declined. So we talked with her slouched there in front of me. "What would you like Santa to bring you?" I asked.
"Nothing".

"I am guessing you would enjoy CD's or new clothes. What is it that you would like?" and I stretched out my hand to her.

"Oh Santa" she sobbed as she sat on my knee and hugged me as tight as she could, "I just want someone to love me"!

My heart broke. I was almost crying myself. This was a fragile moment in a fragile child's life. I had to convey love to her. Somehow that love must transcend normal, human love that had so obviously failed her. I held her close hugging her back.

The room retained its newly gained party atmosphere as she and I quietly shared her anguish. "Santa loves you", I said as I had said so many times that night and for 20 years. I took her arm from around my shoulder and placed a candy cane in it. "Now hold your cane like this so that the curve is at the top pointing up."

As dramatically as I could, I moved my candy cane to meet hers. Touched together in that position, the two canes form a perfect HEART.

"Like this half of the candy cane, God's love is always there for you. It is ready for you to reach out to take it in" I said. "With His love, you can never be alone any more, no matter where you go, no matter how bad it gets. You are special and you ARE LOVED FOREVER".

Her face brightened. Her damp eyes even smiled as her face began to shine and shine. She hugged me again and said, "Thank you so much. I love you. It is so good to say that to someone who understands."

She took her gift bag and her tiny stuffed animal and walked into the group of other kids.

It was my time to leave, but I couldn't resist telling a volunteer that she was a special little girl and hoping he would give her a little extra attention. I walked out of her life then with another, "Ho, Ho, Merry Christmas", but she is never out of my heart. I pray she finds someone on earth to love her someday.

Where are the Reindeer?

The Christmas party is a long expected, long anticipated event in the lives of those who live in nursing homes and extended care facilities. Just having delicious snacks in the middle of the day is enough to make some of them happy. Having Santa come is the "icing on their cake".

I was invited 30 years ago to attend the Christmas parties at a care center near our home. Previously I had visited some members of our parish who lived there. Since I try to give a special moment to staff who care for those I visit, I had gotten to know the staff and directors there. Seeing the special attention I paid to a few of their beloved residents, they asked me to come to the parties and be Santa for all the people who lived there.

It was an enormous undertaking. More than 150 people live in that multi-story facility. Just carrying the candy canes slung in a bag over my shoulder was a heavy proposition. I have never been sorry that I accepted that first of many invitations for I have watched God work miracles there time and time again.

One rainy December Wednesday a lot of years ago, I had visited the residents in groups at their floor parties on the first and second floors, going in to individual rooms only if nurses mentioned someone was too ill to attend the party in the lounge.

Still it was getting later and I was a little tired. My wife was carrying one bag of candy canes to distribute the weight and so that she could guard it from the diabetics who came to search for and steal the candy when my back was turned. Nurse born apple treats were no substitute for candy canes to some party goers.

We were getting off the elevator at the third floor. I knew from previous visits, that those with less mental capacity were housed higher and higher in the facility. This was never an easy floor to visit. As the elevator doors opened, nurses at the station waved and called out to Santa and pointed for me to turn left.

I strode purposely forward to meet the nursing director who would act as my guide for that floor. My wife lifted the bags of candy canes out of the elevator and set them on the floor.

"On Dasher, on Dancer, On Prancer and Vixen, on Comet and Cupid, on Donner and Blixen..." she turned to see who was reciting.

The words were coming from the animated face of a drawn looking woman who was tied with restraints into her wheelchair. Her arm was up and pointing down the hall where I had disappeared to visit others. She was nodding her head and reciting the poem.

Caregivers from all over that floor came to look at her in amazement. Soon she stopped speaking, looked around at each caregiver, smiled at them, then dropped her head to her chest again and was silent.

One of the nurses' aides came over to my wife and said, "Be certain to tell Santa what happened. That lady doesn't know her own name or her children, when they visit but she certainly remembered that Christmas poem."

There is a child in each of us and that child must be the last to leave our minds and our bodies.

We learned a lot about Alzheimer's and dementia that day

Santa Isn't Prejudiced

The uniformed man whispered in my ear, "He thinks it may be beneath his dignity. He doesn't want to actually SIT on your knee, but he thinks it may be inspiring to be photographed with you handing him a candy cane."

I was quite surprised since this political candidate's office had been quite demanding that I should be available for this press conference. He was not the first man who was reluctant to show interest in Santa. Others have thought at first that it might lessen their distinction if they sat on my lap. I couldn't help remembering other such incidents as I waited for the press conference to begin.

I had just come from visiting folks at an office few find pleasurable to visit, the Internal Revenue Service. I was on my way to another office most people avoid whenever possible, the Arizona Department of Revenue.

I have come to know some wonderful, noble, gracious people at both of those offices and they love to have a good time at parties joking with each other and with Santa. Some of them fit the model of "forgotten and alone in a crowd" just like employees of any large organization.

The heads of those agencies have had numerous interactions with Santa over the years.

Many have; sat on Santa's lap, been photographed for company newsletters with their tiny bears and Santa, and encouraged Santa to visit other divisions of their own agencies.

I remembered another day when I had gone to pay a "thank you" visit to a man who helped arrange a personal loan at the bank for me. When I arrived, his co-workers told me that he was in a meeting. I followed the directions to the meeting room and opened the door expecting to see about 8 to a dozen people inside. I can still feel the adrenalin rushing through me as it did that day when I realized I had opened the door near the front of a huge meeting room and about 1000 sets of eyes were now trained on me.

Since I had already caused a monumental interruption of the meeting and since I couldn't think of any other response to the silent speaker and the "Ooh, Santa. Ho, Ho, Ho" coming from the audience. I walked to the podium.

I began to speak to the people gathered about Christmas, about their wonderful customers, urged them to be kinder to their bosses and chastened the bosses to be extra sensitive to their employees and give them praise for the good jobs they do. With a hearty, "Ho, Ho, Merry Christmas" I left to applause and rousing cheers from everyone in the room.

On my way out, I turned to the man who had been speaking to give him a hug and thank him for letting me come in.

He hugged me back to the sound of even louder cheering and a standing ovation from his employees.

I read his nametag. It said, "President of the Bank". He had graciously relinquished his position of power to let me use the microphone and give him a hug.
Now this politician felt his position was in jeopardy if he sat on Santa's knee. Politically, he was not my favorite candidate, but as a man with a stress stretched face who needed a lift from Santa's love, he fit the bill.

I walked over to him, posed for the cameras with a smile and then told him, "Santa loves you, even if you won't sit on his lap. You know I have held people who weighed almost 400 pounds. I know where you can sit on my knee and not hurt either one of us. A mayor, a chief of police, several bishops have all sat on my knee to the delight of their staff and public. Sometimes showing human softness and accepting love shows strength, not weakness to your employees and constituents." He looked thoughtful, but he did not smile.

"Merry Christmas"

His Name is Nicholas?

The little boy's face was so excited. He would lower the car window and wave and turn to tell his father about seeing Santa in the car beside him. His father waved and smiled to me and raised the window of the car. The excited little face was soon looking out of an open window again and he was waving and saying something to me.

I reached for the candy canes I keep near at hand while I am driving so that I can toss them to people who get so excited at seeing me that they forget to drive their cars in a straight line. I have almost been sideswiped many times by excited drivers.

Catching the driver's eye, I showed him the candy canes and motioned for him to pull over into an empty office parking lot in the next block. With hand and head signals, he slowed down and let me precede him in his lane so we could turn into the lot together.

I was busy getting my hat on straight and getting out of the car when two little arms grabbed me around the knees and the little boy was screaming, "It's Santa. It's Santa. Come and see Santa!"

I followed his eyes and saw another car had pulled into the lot with us and more people were piling out and coming over to my car. When young and old, tall and short had received a candy cane, I was able to ask the driver of the first car, "Is this a party? Where are all of you going?"

"To the hospital, he said. My wife is going to have a baby and we are all going with her!"

"Oh my" I thought. "Where is she now?" I asked.

"Oh she is in that first car. That is our little boy who is so excited to see you. It is OK. She said it is OK to stop for a while."

I walked to the car where a sweet faced young woman and a much-concerned older woman sat together watching the 12 or more family members munch candy canes. "Merry Christmas" I said and handed each of them a candy cane. "I do wish you many blessings this night and a safe delivery." She smiled and nodded and I knew her family needed to hurry along.

It took a few minutes and a lot of scrambling to fit everyone into the two cars. I followed them the block and a half to the hospital. As they went into the entrance, the father turned back toward me and said, "We'll name the baby after you, Santa."

What's In a Costume?

"I'll never make it to the gate on time!" I thought as I hurried down the corridor at Sky Harbor Airport. I could see the line waiting at the security area to have their luggage scanned.

"I'm nearly there. Without my pack, I should be able to walk straight through without stopping," I thought.

Just then an entire group of little girls broke away from their leader and ran shrieking across the lobby towards me crying, "Santa. It is Santa!"

"I'll be late for certain" I thought as I bent to pat each little head. I had left my pack in the car knowing I would need to pass security and probably need to help my wife with her carried on gifts and luggage—"If I ever get to meet her" I thought.

I wished that I had the pack or at least a lot of candy canes now. It was hard to pass up the children without giving them any candy.

"No, dear, Santa is not catching a plane. My sleigh and reindeer are waiting to take me around the world on Christmas Eve. I am just going to meet someone at a gate. I need to hurry."

"Merry Christmas." With a pat on the shoulder for their leader who was just coming up to her run-away group, I hurried back out into the stream of moving travelers.

This time it wasn't children who stopped me, but the security guards who wanted to greet me and tell me their wishes for Christmas. "I'll never make it on time" I thought.

People in the oncoming groups of passengers looked tired and burdened with the bags of gifts and luggage they carried until they noticed me. I tried to scan each group in case my wife had left her gate and was coming out alone.

"Merry Christmas" I beamed and waved to them. Most of the weary travelers smiled and straightened up looking refreshed as they passed by.

18, 20, 22, then Gate 24 was in sight. I wanted to be there when she came out of the jet way from the plane. She was tired from her care giving trip to another state. I hoped to cheer her up as I could cheer up others.

"Just in time" I thought as I noticed the first few passengers coming off the plane from Washington, D.C. Quickly I found the perfect seat and just sat down to wait. Sitting it seemed that people did not feel the freedom to interrupt me as they do when I am standing and walking around.

I could see the passengers as they deplaned. At last, I saw my wife. She did look tired. She also looked apprehensive as though she didn't really expect me to be there to meet her.

Santa has a lot of obligations. Maybe there had been too many recently.

I continued to sit a few more seconds while she scanned the arrival lounge. Her eyes passed over me and went to a tall man in the corner. Then she looked back to me and smiled. I grabbed her hand, took her luggage and we walked swiftly out of the terminal with hands swinging talking intently. It was just about the only time I, as Santa Claus, have not been stopped every few feet by well-wishers and "fans".

During that time I was wearing the false beard and wig. 36 years ago when I began as Santa, my hair and beard were dark brown. Over the years nature lightened my hair with silver highlights until now it and my beard are completely gray.

Many years ago I began leaving the false beard and wig in the car for some appearances. Then I let the normally trimmed beard grow until in the 20th season I used the naturally gray beard and hair only.

The grayer and rounder I have gotten, the more often children and adults have mentioned to me that I looked like Santa.

It has been hard to vacation without interruption. Sometimes I could not shop uninterrupted even wearing my regular street clothes.

This year my wife and daughter had to buy the presents for my grandson while I was busy holding two little girls and talking to numerous adults who kept calling me, "Santa" while I shopped.

I guess the image and appearance and demeanor of Santa are pervasive and accepted…even by those closest to me. This year my own adult daughter called me from a fashionable jewelry store and said, "Hi, Dad. I have found what I want for Christmas. Please give this man your credit card number."

"Thanks". "Bye".

A Visit for One Who Has 'Everything'

"My son works so hard. He deserves a lovely break and a happy time when he comes this Christmas. It is hard for him to just go out to parties. He and his wife just had a new baby," she said as she took another deep breath. "Please come."
"I'll pay you anything you ask," she pleaded.

I smiled into the phone, but I couldn't accommodate her request. She was asking for me to visit on Christmas Eve! By then I would have held nearly 5000 people on my lap in December. I would be so tired. My plans for Christmas Eve had been made long ago.

I began as Santa at the Children's service at All Saints' Episcopal Church over 20 years before her call. I continued to be the Santa at that service which concludes at dark. Then I spent time visiting the sick of the parish and rushed home for a quick family dinner of homemade vegetable soup. (My wife learned long ago that soup was necessary to boost my electrolytes and increase my energy to improve my "at home" disposition.)

After dinner I would spend the first evening in weeks quietly at home with my family and my little grandson.
We would read the story of the birth of Jesus from the Bible again and someone would read "T'was the Night Before Christmas" poem.

The great moment would arrive when the young of the household can select one gift to open before bedtime. Oh, the tension, the decisions, the shaking and poking and hinting for clues before the package is chosen! After the gift is open and enjoyed it is time for bed. Then hugs and kisses over and over and yet again.

I enjoy being the real Santa at my house helping fill the stockings and put out the special unwrapped gifts that will excite the little boy grandson when he enters the room Christmas morning. He will know Santa came when he sees the toy that was on his list that he carefully prepared with his grandmother. "Make the list very long, please," he asked as she typed the names of toys from the catalogues he had saved. "I want Santa to know that I need each one."

That first year when he was three he asked, "Do you think my mommy has Santa's FAX number? This list is ready for the FAX". I always wondered what the neighborhood printer's staff thought when that list came out of their machine the first year. Later it became tradition and when it was over, they missed the little boy who had grown too big just like we all do.

No, I couldn't fit in another visit on Christmas Eve.
"I'm sorry" I said, "but as I told you last week, I don't see how I can fit a visit to your family in this Christmas Eve."

"But you understand that I only want you to come because you are the best Santa that I have ever seen."

"Did I tell you that his brother and sister and all their children will be here together on that night? Could you please come?"

My silence must have been discouraging because she continued, "I'll call you tomorrow night in case you can work out something. Please come to make the holiday special for my son. He works so hard. He can come home with his family so seldom. He is such a nice person. You'll like my son. Everyone does. My son is Ricky….." She named a famous child movie star who was still a successful TV and movie star as an adult. It probably was hard for him to come home and it certainly was hard for him to go out to parties to just have fun.

"I'll call you tomorrow night."

I thought about her request in a new light after that call. No, I don't believe I was star struck. I think instead that I was reminded how lonely the rich and successful and important people can feel either because of their success or in spite of it.
  Ricky's mother had told me that she thought I was the best Santa she had ever seen. She had taken her other grandchildren to see Santa at the country club when I was the Santa there.
  I always spent all the time it took for each family grouping of pictures, to listen to each child, to soothe the frightened little one, to let Mommy and Daddy take additional pictures.
  She had noticed that even the little children of wealthy families needed time and attention and love. She wanted that for the rest of her family.

I talked to my wife and daughter. "Your grandson is quite a bit bigger now and can stay up until you get home for the readings and opening his one gift," his mother said.

I called the church and found out that fewer were on the parish sick list and that I had seen most of them already and would have a short visiting list that Christmas Eve.

The next night when she called she began with, "Oh, I hope you've thought about my request to make my son's Christmas the most special it could be. Will you please come to see us?"

When I told her I had arranged to be free, she was delighted and began telling me about each child, about her son's childhood memories of Santa and earlier Christmas visits.
 I took good notes because it always helps to know a few facts in case someone is skeptical when presented with Santa Claus.

We arranged that she would leave a big bag of gifts for each child outside the door in the evening. I would come to the walkway, put her bag of gifts into my red velvet bag so that I could pull out a specific gift for each one when I was inside.

My wife went with me to take pictures and to carry my second bag. It is so difficult to see when wearing the costume beard and wig that she was helping me look for the bag of gifts. We looked and looked and finally began to laugh. The entire walkway was lined with big boxes that were gift wrapped! We had lifted several and realized they were just decorations before we began to despair that we would not detect the real gifts.

Closer to the doorway, behind a little shrub, was a huge bag with many little gifts inside. We were relieved to find them.

The children were beautiful in their matching nightgowns and pajamas, all 7 of them; the tree was 15 feet high with gorgeous decorations, the fire burned brightly with chestnuts roasting (yes, really) and our celebrity was having a wonderful time holding his children on his lap in his bare feet, questioning Santa about how he knew so much about him.

The children got cute presents from Santa's bag and just before I left, I leaned over to Ricky and whispered another little story courtesy of his mother.

"How can you know all of this?" he questioned.

"I told you, I am Santa Claus, and I love you and all your children." He gave me a little hug.

His mother sent a check to the church as her appreciation for our visit. She told me it was the highlight of their Christmas together. The visit was gratifying to me, too, to see that parents love their children and grandchildren whether they are rich or poor, celebrity or of humble means.

There was not a Humbug in sight.

Children's Comments and Truths

"Santa, remember that I have moved to 4554 North Club Street now! Don't take my presents to that other house, please!"

Children know that Santa visits every child in the world on the same night distributing toys and candy to delight their hearts. American children believe that Santa makes all the toys at the North Pole throughout the year. Sometimes they believe other things, too, and I have to be quick thinking to respond to them without disturbing their beliefs.

Phoenix doesn't have snow, even at Christmas. I drive a car or a van loaded with candy and stuffed animals to distribute to the children and adults I see. "Where are your reindeer, Santa?" comes annually. I answer with great seriousness, "The reindeer work very hard on Christmas Eve so they are resting now to be able to pull that heavy sleigh when the time comes. They are very shy and you may not ever see them. They are magic, you know."

"How big is the sleigh?

"Big enough to hold the toys and presents. Don't worry about that" I say assuredly.

"Can the reindeer pull the sleigh without snow?"

"Oh yes, the sleigh flies and doesn't need snow. A lot of the world is desert like Phoenix and Santa finds a way to visit all of the children."

"Why does Santa need a watch?"
"It is a very special watch. Do you see my picture on the dial? That means it tells me the time wherever I need to go to see other boys and girls. Some children like you get a special visit from Santa before Christmas. Santa doesn't like to keep you and your parents waiting so I look at the time in Phoenix."

"How many elves do you have, Santa? How big are they, really?"

"The elves are about your size," I say, "and it takes a lot of them to make all those toys. You should take their example to heart and be certain to stay in school a long time. The elves go to college to get degrees in engineering and become scientists and inventors so they can make all those electronic toys you ask me to bring. Things change fast in this world today. You have to study to keep up. Take a lesson from the elves. You will grow taller than they are, but never forget how smart they are."

"Why is my stuffed animal squashed, Santa?"

"Oh dear. Look at that bent ear. You know all those animals ride around in my velvet bag.

 They get to know each other very well and so they play and romp around together inside the bag when I am not looking. Sometimes they get a little bent for a while. Let's just fix your animal so he looks new again."

"That beard is FAKE!"
"Oh, now don't tell everyone the secret," I whisper. "You are right that this long fluffy white beard is the best fake beard I can find. Please give me your hand. I am going to let you feel something and then you will know the secret."

Gently, I lift their hand underneath the false whiskers up to my chin. The look on their faces is filled with wonder and surprise. They can feel the real beard underneath!

"You are feeling my real beard," I explain. "I have to keep it cut quite short during the year because I work so hard making the toys. Can you imagine how bad a long beard would look full of paint and wood chips? I keep my real beard short to keep it clean. Children expect Santa to have a clean white beard and they like it to be LONG, too. I put on this fake beard to make them happy. It is a secret. Don't tell your little brother and sister."

They slide happily off my lap and always turn back to wave to me before they run to their parents to show their gift.

"How will you get into my house to leave my presents? We don't have a fireplace or a chimney and my Dad won't buy one."

"There is a special key that I carry on Christmas Eve that works for the roofs of houses without fireplace chimneys. The key only works on Christmas Eve, however, and I have the only one, of course."

They look quite relieved, secure in the knowledge that there is a way for me to bring their toys.

"You were late this afternoon. If you were late, how do we know you can find us when it is really important, like on Christmas Eve?"

"My GPS guidance system wasn't working too well today. The elves are working on fixing that and assure me that it will be in perfect working order by Christmas Eve. Don't worry, I'll find you."

When children see me in the grocery store or doctor's office or other unexpected place, I remind them, "Santa is always watching."

"How do you know if I am naughty or nice? My friend was really bad last year and he got a bike!"

Thankfully, God is with me, giving me inspiration and love even when the beautiful kids are not acting very nice or are threatening to mess up my velvet with sticky fingers.

"Santa and your parents want you to be the best little boy or girl that you can be. We want you to love God, go to school, help at home and always be kind. We also know that we can't always do the right thing even when we want to. That is why God sent Jesus to be born on Christmas Day. Jesus came to forgive us when we do bad things. We don't always understand why we are good today and not good tomorrow. Certainly we can never understand the same things about someone else. The best thing is to worry only about our own place on the good kids' list, not someone else's."

Miracle in Your Own Home

Strange as it may sound, I was outside in the rain ringing my own front doorbell. I was quite excited and wondering just what reception I would get from the one designated that night to open the door. He was almost three years old, and he knew who brings the toys to "good little boys".

I could look through the clear sidelight windows of the door and see him coming to the door urged on by his mother. When he saw me through the window, he stopped dead in his tracks. I waved to him. He waved weakly, shyly, back to me. Again his mother urged him to the door. At last the door opened and I could say to my own grandson, "Merry Christmas, Johnathan".

He stepped aside finally to let me come in out of the dark and the rain and I asked if I could come to sit down. He took me to the living room and I chose a sofa for my seat. I had taken 2 large wrapped gifts from his mother and grandmother and placed them into my velvet bag when I left home. Now was the time to make my long awaited presentation of the first personal gift from Santa to this special little boy.

"Johnathan, come sit on my lap", I encouraged. Without hesitation he climbed up. He leaned back to survey me carefully. I was still uncertain of my acceptance. He was uncertain, too.

It was time to reach into the bag on the floor beside me and pull out the first wrapped gift. Johnathan knew what that meant! The gift was for him. He took the present and tore off the wrapping quickly as little children do and looked briefly at the box. Then he turned to show his present to his mother and grandmother who were quite busy taking video and pictures of the event. When I took the second gift from my bag, he was watching carefully where my hand had gone. He took off the wrapping, opened the box inside, said "Thank you", showed his mother and hopped down off my lap.

None of us was exactly sure what he was thinking now, but it wasn't long before we knew without a doubt. He was headed to the flat velvet bag on the floor. Before we knew it he had the top pulled over his little head and was feeling around inside. At least a hundred children had done exactly that during the years before.

It is a "magic" bag, you see. It must be because all the toys come from there. Johnathan was no different. Hadn't two packages for him just come from there? He wondered if there was an endless supply and wanted to see how many more gifts there might be for him.

Just as soon as he determined that the velvet bag was empty for now, he came back to me and took my hand. Now, instead of leading me to the living room, he was leading me...pulling me TO THE FRONT DOOR!

Yes, I was being shown the door of my own home by my own grandson...in no uncertain terms.

Being a gracious guest, I left with a hearty, "Ho, Ho, Ho, Merry Christmas". Walking around the front of the house to the garage, I wondered what to do. We had planned my first visit so carefully, but not beyond the point of the gift giving.

Johnathan and his mother had lived in our home most of his tiny life. He knew me quite well. We had planned for his mother to take him out in the car before I dressed as Santa for the first time that year. Thinking he would not remember I had been Santa in his earlier years, he would see me tonight during his own visit from Santa. We hadn't wanted to ruin the belief in Santa that young children have just because a Santa's helper lived in his own home. It had worked beautifully until now. What should I do? As I walked, I realized that I was too tired to drive away and come back later. I had to face coming home when "Santa" had just been thrown out. It had to be now.

I took off my beard and wig and unlocked the back door. Then I came in the back door wearing only the suit and jingly boots and called out, "Hi everyone, I'm home".

Johnathan came running up to me with his arms up. I picked him up and he looked at me shyly for a minute and then he showed me his new toys...from Santa.

I was accepted again as his grandfather.

(Johnathan believed in Santa Claus as other children do until he was 9 years old. We had feared the lovely myth would last less time for him than for other children raised in normal households. We believe that all our activity to prepare happiness and gifts for others for Christmas , and the feeling of the joy of Jesus' coming at Christmas kept his belief alive even longer than for other children.

My bringing in wrapped gifts his mother had hidden in the garage for him, when I came home from being Santa didn't hurt his belief, either.

Could it be true? "You must believe, if you want to receive!"

Who are the Forgotten?

The notes of "Santa Claus is Coming to Town" preceded me into the large hotel convention center decorated lavishly for the company Christmas party. The band was given a break after my introduction and I began to give out the corporate gifts.

Each one was beautifully wrapped. Each one was identical for every woman and man--Corporate logo on a gold jewelry item. One by one the employees came to sit on my lap and each one maintained their corporate demeanor throughout the acceptance of their gift. It didn't take long to go through 70 or so gifts as coolly accepted as they had been coolly given. The party director in her gray suit came to tell me that was enough and I could go. The people had returned to their seats and were quietly talking in little groups. Some put on their coats and seemed ready to go, but were hesitant to know if it would be perceived by someone that they were leaving too soon.

The atmosphere was so cold. The smiles looked forced. The painted faces seemed false and tired. I just moved my chair back towards the wall so the band could get to their seats and gestured to a woman who was looking at me for her to come back up to see me.

She wasn't sure if she should. She glanced back where she had been sitting for guidance from the seatmates, but they were occupied and didn't notice. Then she shrugged her shoulders and came back up to see me.

I asked her about herself. What service she provided to the company. Did she have a family? Where would she spend Christmas? Before long she was smiling and telling me about herself and her coworkers. Then she stopped. She said, "Wait just a minute. I think I see her. I'll be back."

In a minute I could see her bringing a beautiful woman back up the aisle, holding her by the hand...dragging her almost. She pushed her towards me and I held out my hand to her. Gingerly she sat on the end of my knee, stiffly as if she was too heavy. When I asked her to tell me about herself, she barely spoke and remained rigid. I gave her another candy cane and she turned toward me finally to receive it. Gradually she began to relax a bit and tell me a funny story about her friend who had brought her up to see me. Then without a pause, she started to sob.

It was the first time I had ever had someone ask me for a husband. She needed a husband. She was so lonely. She was truly beautiful, poignant, sweet and lonely.
I told her I could not promise, but that if she would try letting other people see this side of her, I believed that by next year I would have good news for her.

Walking the corridors between cubicles in offices and visiting at company parties, I have learned that there are many lonely people in the midst of the crowds around them. They live in secret fear that there is nothing more to life than the lonely working hours where they live in the constant threat of being "downsized" or "right sized" or "laid off". If they look for more in life, they look in other lonely places like bars and singles clubs.

Lonely people aren't always obvious. She was just the first of many successful, beautiful, secretaries and executives who have told me they feel alone, hopeless, and afraid.

As Santa, I assure them that I love them. I tell them that many churches are happy, safe places to be where they can find other people with similar ideas and a place to learn more about Jesus, the Reason for the Season.

I make sure to show people, especially the lonely ones, the candy cane heart. Two candy canes, held horizontally touching at their bases, when moved towards each other at the top, curved end, form a perfect heart. This is Jesus' heart. Every time you see a candy cane for the rest of your life, you will remember that God and Jesus love you.

May God continue to bless you.

Andre House

Homeless children learn quickly not to trust strangers —
especially adult strangers. Authorities take children from
parents who do not provide shelter and food regularly for their
children. Other poor or mentally ill people living on the streets
take their toys or even their food. Little children quickly learn to
hide and learn the places to go when hiding is not possible.

Andre House provides dinner each evening for those who live
for that night at the Phoenix City shelter. People line up to
receive the soup or sandwich and fruit that are dispensed from
the back of trucks by volunteers from various churches in the
city. The soup is made daily from whatever has been donated
and chopped by volunteers who take a few hours from work to
cook and distribute dinner.

This Christmas Santa was at the Andre House annual party for
families who have been "adopted for gifts" by individuals and
churches. I was hoping to bring a little happiness and trust into
the lives of these children from the streets. The story of how this
Santa got to the doors serving the poorest of the poor begins with
some of the richest in town.

This volunteer Santa has been auctioned by charities many times to help them raise money for their mission. We prepare a sign with my picture and copies of the newspaper articles about some of the places I have been. The auction item includes a 2-hour visit for a party of up to 100 people complete with gift giving and stories.

This fall I had agreed to be part of a very fancy charity event and to help with promoting the silent auction by appearing live on TV news several times and encouraging those in attendance to bid on all the items up for auction. Almost everyone enjoyed joking with Santa about their early Christmas shopping and the bids kept going up.

There was a baby about 15 months old who attended this fancy dinner. His doting grandparents had connections to the charity board and loved Santa, but the baby just screamed whenever I walked too near him. Throughout the evening as the parents and grandparents went about their bidding and socializing, I would smile at the baby or offer him a candy cane.

Eventually he stopped screaming and just turned his head away when I came too near.

During dinner he became curious because he sat at the table next to ours. Even though I was out of costume eating my own dinner, he would come over to look at me before being snatched back to his chair by a careful parent.

As we left the posh hotel, we learned that his grandparents had paid a lot of money to buy the Santa visit I had offered to the charity.

At another charity auction my visit had been purchased and given to the fanciest country club in Phoenix area. I went one year and was always invited to go back because I took plenty of time with each child and family.

The week before I went to Andre House this year courtesy of the little baby's grandfather, I went back to the country club that gives a nice donation to our church to help defray the costs of the Santa ministry. As I arrived at the door, a tiny girl came rushing to meet me.

I stooped down to greet her, picked her up and carried her into the meeting room with me as I made my way through the eager children and adults to my seat on the stage. She had her gift, her candy cane, her visit with Santa and lots of pictures taken. It was a nice visit with her and the other children all dressed in their finest velvets and taffeta.

As soon as I stepped into the room at Andre House and took my seat in preparation to greet the homeless children, a lady about my age jumped onto my lap. She did not have the appearance of being homeless. Instead she looked quite nice. I was a little surprised until she said, "You are the best Santa in the whole world!"
"I saw you last week".

"Where did you see me"? I asked.

"At the country club" she said.

"Do you remember the little girl who ran to greet you as you arrived at the club that afternoon?

"I remember the cute little girl I carried into the meeting room," I said.

"She is my granddaughter," she said "and there is so much more to the story! You see, she was so afraid of Santa Claus whenever he was on television or anywhere. We didn't know what to expect when we brought her to the club for the party. When she ran to you, we were all surprised. Then you knelt down to talk to her and she let you pick her up!" she exclaimed.

"We got wonderful pictures of her and you were so patient with her and with our picture taking! We just wanted you to know that you are the best Santa in the world. I am so glad you are here at Andre House. We are on the Board of Directors here and are so happy you have come."

Lift for the Helpers

"This is a private meeting." "Please ask at the front desk for directions to where you need to be."

"I know this is private," I said. "That is why I have brought presents here for each of you."

I shifted the bulging red velvet bag that hung against my back, bringing it out where each one could see it. "It will take more than this to lift their spirits", I thought, "for they surely seem unhappy".

The private meeting was in a hospital. It was a meeting of social workers, those special people who soothe and smooth out processes and care giving for those in poor health. These are the very people whose job it is to cheer and comfort patients and their families while one is admitted to the hospital and even after they are discharged to go home. These people are trained for six or seven years to evaluate patient needs and find the hospital or community services they need for the most efficient and complete care while they are ill.

The continuing education program for their December meeting was in progress when I walked into the room with my "Merry Christmas" and jingling boots. Only one of the social workers smiled at me with a greeting.

"Hi Santa. Come in.," she said. She had invited me. I was her surprise gift for her friends and colleagues. I was bringing her specially selected gifts to each social worker and the speaker. She had worked quite hard devising a plan to cheer up these overburdened, exhausted, and depressed women. She spent her own money and time with their gifts and then she wrote a little history of each lady for me so that I could personalize each gift presentation. I was looking forward to this "assignment" because her unusually thorough efforts had prepared me for the personal distribution of presents.

"Thank you, Barbara," I said because I knew most of the other names, too. "I am so glad you are together today because it makes it easier for me to deliver your gifts." I took a chair up to the front of the room, totally usurping the position of the speaker who wasn't completely sure how to respond.

Barbara gently led her to a chair and told her it would be all right to continue later. The Jewish speaker didn't look convinced, but tried to remain polite.

I told the group of social workers how much we appreciate the jobs they perform for the sick. I explained that I see about 5000 people personally each December and most of them are ill at home, in hospitals and nursing homes. I always notice nurses' aides and others caring for patients.

"I rarely see you, the social workers, however, because you have done your job and gone".

Then I reached into my bag and began to pull out a gift for each one. I called them one at a time to sit on my knee as I made the presentation of each gift with personal comments and questions about their lives. Each one was so surprised when I knew something about her. Their surprise delighted the others until the room was exploding with laughter and excitement.

From throwing me out the door, they had turned into women with barely contained anticipation for the next gift to come out of the bag.

The expression on the face of the Jewish speaker was priceless when I called her name. She didn't know whether to disavow knowledge of Santa or to come openly as others were doing. (The gifts were lovely, special items.) Finally curiosity won and she came and even sat on my knee to receive her gift.

"I wonder how I will ever capture their interest again after this," she said.

Just before I left, I showed them the candy cane heart. I asked them to make a heart of love with each other by joining their own candy cane to that of someone else. "Just remember, Santa loves you."

"Jesus always loves you", I said.

When I left the room a few minutes later, it was filled with uplifted, happy, joyous women who could return to their jobs with lighter hearts and sincere smiles.

E R

My call that night just before Christmas was for me to come. "Would you come to the ICU please?" my friend asked. "We brought my father here. He is in a lot of pain, but you remember how much he and Mother always enjoy seeing Santa when they come for Christmas."

My Santa suit was already on and I made certain to have enough time that evening to visit that hospital ICU. I have been in many hospitals over the years and except for the actual sterile operating rooms, I have never been denied access to any area. I just walk up to the keypad doorways, knock and wave. Whoever monitors the door opens it and greets me with a wave and a "Come on in, Santa."

I've walked into the helipad, suture rooms, radiology, dialysis, labor and delivery, oncology and Intensive Care. I admit I walk more slowly in there so the bells jingle a little more softly. The nurses wave merrily and are very happy I have come to see their patient. I only stay a moment, offer a candy cane, a touch, and a stuffed animal.

That night I was there for the family. The father was too ill to notice me, but his elderly wife certainly gave me a big hug. She slipped a tiny teddy bear under her husband's hand and patted it gently, then smiled at me. Their son, my friend, was glad I had come.

As I turned to leave, a nurse came up to me and entreated me to come with her to the Emergency Room. She had just brought a patient up to ICU and had to hurry back because the ER was crowded.

We've all seen the TV show. Most of us have been to the Emergency Room ourselves or with a loved one. It was the first time I had been escorted there by a nurse.

That night in the Phoenix hospital would have challenged the writers of any TV show. There were sick people in every cubicle, in the hallways, parked along the nursing station partition and anywhere else barely within the double doors that say, "Keep Out".

That sensitive nurse took me up to a procedure room where stitches were being placed and left me as she was called to another duty. The doctor inside motioned me in and I greeted the bleeding patient with a "Merry Christmas". "Santa loves you. Take better care of yourself next year, please."

As I turned around I could see bleeding and scared people looking at me from gurneys and wheelchairs. I couldn't just walk away from them. I gave out over 50 animals that night and many more candy canes as I went from stretcher to stretcher, cubicle to cubicle greeting and touching the sick and hurt people. Most of them smiled at me and brightened for a while before their focus returned to their suffering.

Before I left, I made a special point to stop each technician, each nurse and doctor I could find and give them a hug, a candy cane, and an animal...stressing that the toy was for them--the caregiver to remember that Santa and Jesus love them. They were the heroes and heroines that night keeping lives and skin and bones together...always running full speed ahead.

The TV writers and Michael Crichton, producer of ER haven't even imagined what happens in our real ER's.

SANTA WITHOUT A SLEIGH?

"Thank you Santa. It was a pleasure meeting you even in June under these circumstances. I hope you have a nice trip." The tired young woman smiled as I got out of my first class seat on my way to the airplane door at my destination 14 hours late. I thanked the flight attendant, sent a quick message to our pilot thanking him for a safe landing and then turned to hurry out the door ahead of the throng behind me who had heard the "ding" when the door had opened.

My next hour was hectic. I was racing to secure my rental car before the office closed for the holiday, racing to claim luggage from an airport carousel doubled up with luggage from two flights because ours was so late arriving, then racing to find the highway for the 3 hour drive to the bride's home before everyone praying for our safe flight had gone to bed, and giving up on finding any supper so late. After about an hour of driving, I turned to my wife and asked, "How are you?"

"I'm just fine now that we are on the right road" she said. She looked tired, but she wasn't nervous--just a little hungry.

"I think God had a plan for us on that plane today" I ventured. "I am glad His plan included helping other people and that we lived to complete it."

I am used to finding myself in situations where I am God's messenger to hurting people while I am wearing the red velvet Santa suit in December. I am not used to such intense encounter as we had had this day in June.

Just after we had taken off for a non-stop flight from Phoenix to St. Louis enroute to a family wedding, flight attendants snatched our beverages and snack bags from us and told us to belt tightly and brace for an emergency landing in Albuquerque. Bouncing around in the sky I looked below and saw only desolate New Mexico desert. When I had finished praying, I looked at my wife and saw that she had been praying, too. Through her tears she whispered that she was glad I was with her, but very sorry that I had decided to accompany her after all.

"You could have lived years longer if you hadn't come on this flight," she said.

We held hands and smiled knowing that after 38 years of being married we would face whatever was ahead together.

In a few minutes, my wife said to me, "Just look at that young mother up there and smile encouragingly, please. Now. She keeps looking back at you." I knew just who she meant. Her husband was seated beside me, but he was reading a newspaper. She and their baby were alone in the seat in front of him.

Her eyes were wide, wide open with fear and were ringed with tears about to cascade down her cheeks. She was not speaking. I knew she did not want to alarm the peaceful baby by having her voice crack, but she was turned almost all the way around in that coach seat with fear and pleading in her eyes.

I did look over at her. I smiled in what I hoped was an encouraging way. Then I mouthed the words, "It will be OK." She seemed relieved and settled down in her seat for a few minutes.

The head flight attendant announced, "The pilot is quite busy now, but he wants you to know that although one engine is turned off, the other seems to be functioning fine. Remain in your seats."

The young girl in the seat in front of us turned around to talk. She was chattering but peaceful. We learned she had a deep faith in God and although she didn't say so, she just wanted to be connected to someone during our bouncy flight. Her seat companion was a stranger to her and he was drunk.

We had an exciting, but safe, landing in Albuquerque and left the plane to rest in the lounge while the engine problem was diagnosed. "Forty minutes is all" the ground attendants keep saying for several hours. By now, the passengers had talked to the media, finally talked to each other a little, noticed those who were too afraid to ever get back on the plane, and realized that the words "forty minutes" just meant "in a little while--maybe".

At last we boarded the plane again and were ready to back away from the gate when a horrible dust storm came leaving visibility at zero. We stayed put. It was disconcerting sitting there with the plane bouncing and swaying in the violent gusts of swirling wind. Someone began to cry so I said, "I'm from the desert. These just last a few minutes. It'll be over soon!" Nobody answered. We just sat silently and listened to the wind whistling.

At last we began to taxi. The flight attendants showed us the emergency exits and asked us to look at the emergency cards located in the seat pockets in front of us. Most of us paid a lot more attention to her instructions this time than we had before the last flight.

Just before we made the turn onto the runway to take off our pilot announced,

"We are taking another precaution and returning to the gate for mechanics to investigate our engines again." The 15-minute taxi began and some passengers began to unload their items from the overhead bins. Some of them had had enough stress and were leaving the plane for good.

This time we were asked not to leave the plane at the gate. My wife and I stayed in our seats in the silence until I needed to stretch.

I stood up and made a small remark to the lady behind me who was crying. She smiled a bit and said to me, "I thought you were probably a nice man. You look so much like Santa Claus!"

I smiled and my wife whispered that our small photo album was in her carry on luggage…top right she motioned. I lifted the luggage down and still talking to the teary lady I handed the photo album to her opened to a picture of me in the red suit.

"You are Santa!" she said. She handed the album to the people across the aisle from her. I handed my business card that says "Santa Claus" to the man beside me. Soon people were asking questions about Santa.

I stayed standing and relayed stories different people told loudly to the others in the coach section. Someone told a joke. Someone else relayed it to the others. There was laughter and exchange of stories.

Our books and reading material had been finished sometime during the previous 8-hour wait. No one seemed to want to sleep. We became friends, then cohorts, and then family.

It had gotten hot even though it was long dark. We were into our third hour on the plane the second time. We were uncomfortable, but trying to have a good time when the flight attendant came to me and asked me to follow her into first class section.

I had noticed the weeping girl before. The flight attendants had been trying to calm her for hours. She had moved to first class to be more comfortable because she was sick. Actually our delay getting to St Louis and missing flight connections to destinations all over the world for our accompanying passengers could be costing her her life. She was flying to Philadelphia for an appointment with a medical specialist who could answer her life or death question about treatment. The tired flight attendant asked if I would just talk with her.

As I sat and looked at her she folded and unfolded a long cosmetic case filled with more medication bottles than I have seen outside a pharmacy. I was worried for her, but I decided to just be friendly and hopeful. We talked about 20 minutes and she had stopped crying. Soon she asked if I was the Santa Claus?

I showed her my album, and then we passed it around the first class section. Some of those passengers had been afraid, too, but did not join us in the "coach luggage" section laughing and joking session. Now they relaxed a bit and actually talked to each other!

14 hours late we finally took off for St. Louis…in the same plane that had had two major mechanical problems in the same day. We had lost some frightened passengers who had left the plane, but most of us stayed aboard and flew forward in faith. The stewardess began her spiel about the safety features on the card located in the seatback in front of us. Then she shrugged and said, "After 3 times today, I guess you already know all of that" and she sat down.

My wife and I were invited to larger seats in first class for the rest of the flight in payment for the reassurance we had given to so many frightened people. We were tired. Babies fretted. People talked with their seatmates. The airline gave us pretzels. We landed safely—just late, very late.

God is good. We were always in His care, but some people didn't know that or forgot in their fear. Their trust in the folk hero, Santa Claus, enabled them to relax and endure the stress and discomfort of our "foiled flight" without reindeer.

Not Everyone Loves Santa

"Get out. I told you to get out and don't ever come back in here!" the woman shouted at the top of her voice. Her back was still to me and she sat in the chair watching the blank television set that dominated her sitting room. The nursing assistant who was with me on the tour of the nursing home just shrugged and said, "Thank you for trying. I am not surprised at her behavior, but I was hoping she would let someone come in to see her. It has been a long time since she has seen anyone."

I was touring the nursing home that is next door to our church. For all of the years I have been Santa Claus I have visited the patients and staff there. The first year I was on my way into the church for the Christmas Eve service when I heard their chain link fence rattling. The patients wanted me to come in, but I told them I needed to be in the church service. I promised that I would come back if they would tell their nurses to let me in. I had only candy canes to give them that first year, but they were excited and happy in their pictures with Santa.

This year will be the 37th time Santa will have been at their Christmas parties. The managers, patients, owners and staff have changed over and over again throughout the years, but my name is passed down to the new regime and I am able to continue my visits.

The "Gardens" is a locked facility for those who are unable to walk about freely without being lost or hurt. There are people of various ages and degrees of disability there, but all are quite needy.

Our church members purchase gifts for each patient according to their needs at Christmas. Parishioners take a name from a tree like the "angel trees" in the mall, purchase the gift and return it wrapped for me to deliver to the patients at their Christmas party. Extra sweets, punch and music have all the patients who are able to travel to the dining room smiling and happy when I get there. There are always quite a few patients who are unable to join the party, however, so I visit them individually in their rooms.

Their campus is built like an open school with rooms that open to the outside to sidewalks rather than to interior hallways. The perimeter is fenced and even Santa has to be properly identified before the gate lock is released for him to enter or exit, even in the rain.

After the party dies down a bit, I take the gifts for those who cannot attend and walk down the sidewalks with an aide to show me where each one lives. I talk to them in their beds or chairs and deliver the wrapped gift, the little animal from North Pole ministries and a candy cane hoping our efforts have brightened their day.

There is a building with small apartments instead of the normal sized rooms throughout the rest of the facility. Usually more mobile residents have the apartments and enjoy a life less like a nursing home. They are usually at the party so this day the visit to an apartment was my first. The nurse's aide said, "We all talked about this visit. She is a new resident and she doesn't want to be here. She won't talk to anyone or let anyone in to help her. She is rude, nasty, and sometimes even curses the ones who bring her trays. We thought you might make a difference to her. Do you mind trying?"

I didn't mind trying and so I knocked on the door. The aide pushed the glass door aside and I walked about 2 feet into the sitting room with bells jingling. "Get out!" she said over and over.

"I'm going to leave you," I said, "but I wanted to tell you that Santa loves you and Jesus loves you. I am leaving a candy cane and your present from All Saints Church here on the table by the door. I hope you enjoy them. Merry Christmas".

With a "Ho, Ho, Ho Merry Christmas" I tried to drown out her indignant shouts of "Get Out!"

I tried to reassure the young aide that I was not offended in the least, but I admit that it was a new experience for me to be thrown out when I was Santa Claus.

I'm not sure I would have let a stranger in a costume in my front door, but that is what at least a hundred people have done over the years. Sometimes when I am ahead of schedule and I drive into a neighborhood where there is a party, I walk up to the front window and just stand looking into the party. Soon, someone spots me and with squeals of excitement point that Santa is there.

The host or hostess comes to the door and invites me in. I don't take my bag with me, just a handful of candy canes lest anyone fear I am there for illicit activities. I doubt most of them notice because they are inviting me in and welcoming me like I was the honored guest. The funniest part is how the adults continue to whisper the question in my ear, "Who are you?", as they look around the room to see who might be missing.

Since I don't know anyone at the party, it is really fun to watch them speculate about who invited me and who I might be under the costume. Now that I wear my own beard and no longer have the costume hair I am more recognizable, but for years I would assure the host that no one there knew me. Still, none of them ever threw me out.

The angry lady lived in that apartment for a number of years. Each year I walked down the sidewalk to her apartment, ankle bells ringing. I would knock on her door, stick my head inside and ask permission to come in.

"Get OUT!" she would yell at me over and over again. "I told you last year not to come here again. Get OUT!"

"I'll just leave this candy cane on your table for later. Remember that I love you. Merry Christmas!" I would tell her each year as I turned away from her door.

One year there was quite a surprise at her apartment, however. By now I knew the way to her door and aides no longer accompanied me. I walked jingling to the door, knocked, and asked permission to come inside.

"Oh, I see it is you again," she said indignantly as though I knocked on her door every week or so instead of once a year. "I need help opening this box."

Even with a welcome like that I was glad for a chance to step inside her apartment. I could see she had been struggling with the package. There were scissors and a screwdriver, but the box was not open. As I examined the filament tape holding it together I reached for my keys hoping they would help tear the filaments. "Oh, is this from your son?" I asked her.

"Yes, it is. He usually sends such a small box, but this one is quite large and heavy. He lives so far away that I am surprised he would ship such a box so far."

"I think I can get it open right here." I said. "You must be very excited to see what he has sent for you. Do you think it is your Christmas presents?"

"Yes, I believe it is" she said. Then she looked me in the eye for the first time and said clearly and purposely, "Thank you for helping me. No one else helps me."

We talked a bit more about Christmas and I was able to hand her her first candy cane and animal in all those years. As I said "Goodbye, Merry Christmas!" I asked her if I could come back to see her.

"I think so," she said, "as long as it is not too often."

The administrators and aides told me all year that she was much more agreeable. She didn't throw everyone out the door before they could get in to assist her. Someone said that her son was thinking of coming for a visit. Her life was taking positive steps forward.

I went back to visit the Christmas party the following year, hoping a little that she had continued to progress and would actually attend the party. When I didn't see her, I asked an aide if she was in the same apartment intending to go to see her.

Sadly she had died the previous week. The executive director heard me ask about her, however, and told me again that her last year was so much happier for her and for the staff.

"Her life began to turn around that day you went into her apartment. She talked about Santa Claus often all year. Do you remember that package from her son?" she asked.

"Yes, I do. Opening that package was the first chance I had to actually talk with her or see any of her except her back after all those years."

"She and her son had been estranged for many years and she hadn't heard from him most years. She was very excited to receive the box, but she would accept no help opening it until you came. Whatever he sent to her, helped their relationship improve, too. It was a wonderful year."

God always has a plan, even though we don't understand it. Sometimes we are the very key person to make His plan work, if we are agreeable.

Miracle of the Barbies

It was a bitterly cold December night and I couldn't find a parking place. Throngs of people were wound around the building, an old converted firehouse, and cars were everywhere. My wife was quite disturbed when I followed a limousine up onto the sidewalk to park. I wasn't too worried because I had seen a city of Phoenix police officer wave the big car up onto the walkway.

We had followed the Mayor of the City and the police chief was there to greet him. He assured Santa that there would be no ticket on that night for illegally parking my "sleigh".

Press was everywhere with "live" trucks turning the night into daylight so that the local celebrities arriving could be filmed and introduced by television reporters. I stopped and waved as one of the celebrities because who can give a Christmas party for kids without Santa?

The event was the first big event for a group called Mothers Against Gangs. What a worthy cause. Politians and pastors were escorted to the front of the new "Kids Center" in the converted fire station. My wife and I were escorted to the back room that was nearly filled with toys...huge numbers of toys, games, colorful plaques with children's themes (provided by a generous donation to Santa), new stuffed animals we had brought and another huge bin of "gently used" stuffed animals waiting for a new home.

There was another set of tables stacked high above and below with dolls of every shape, size and color.

My wife took a lot of pictures at first as the children were brought inside from the cold. Soon however, she realized that the number of children and gifts was overwhelming the volunteers, so she pitched in to help with gift location and distribution.

About this time the doors to the front room of the fire station opened. Back to the children...

I was sitting in the middle of the room and after listening intently to the gift requests from each child, I motioned for them to see a lady at the tables. Before long the line of children had become endless to me and I kept sending children to the tables.

My wife had noticed that little girls who wanted dolls were happy with any baby doll we gave them. Some of the dolls, all new in boxes, were as big as the little girls. But as soon as the child's Mom saw the doll, if it was the wrong color, she brought it back to exchange for a doll of the skin color she wanted. Due to the constant exchanges, the doll area became a bit mixed up.

Then an official volunteer announced to the helpers that they were out of Barbie dolls. Even "Barbie like" dolls were gone. My wife came over and whispered in my ear, "Don't promise any more Barbie. We are out. Thanks."

But somehow as I lifted and listened to the endless line of children, I continued to gesture to the tables of dolls when the girls wanted Barbie. .Each time I had promised a Barbie and the trusting little girl had gone to the volunteer to convey Santa's promise, someone found a little stack of Barbie's behind bigger dolls. Each time my wife would notify me when that newfound stack was gone.

Three times my wife came to remind me there were no more Barbie dolls. Three times someone found a small stack of Barbie's in a corner, under the table or behind other dolls. Then my wife, Ellen, made her own exhaustive search for Barbie. She found four more and she was certain that those were the last four in the building that night.

Not wanting to disappoint any children, especially ones who were coming in with their cheeks red from waiting in the cold almost two hours, my wife approached me once again.

"Santa, these are the LAST Barbie's we have", she said in her sternest wifely tone. I thought I got the message this time, but there was still an endless line waiting. Mariachi music was playing in the outdoor food area where a small dinner was served those who had come. Little girls were still wanting baby dolls and of course, Barbie.

I lost count. I had seen the last four dolls. I kept on telling the children to go to the tables for their requests. Two more times the volunteers found stacks of Barbie in corners, under coats, in boxes and amazing places. My wife swore they had not been there when she had searched. The head official volunteer swore and affirmed that the Barbie's had run out.

When the very last little girl in line came to sit on my lap, she looked up with beautiful eyes shining with excitement and trust and said, "Santa, all I want for Christmas is a Barbie."

I gestured to the decimated doll table and the volunteers who had not gone home waiting to see what would happen. They all turned and looked at the last, the very last stack of Barbie's they had found. One doll was left. One little girl was very happy.

No one can explain how Barbie kept reappearing. Other toys ran out. Other dolls were ignored or exchanged.

Somehow, God was showing his concern for little girls that night and multiplied the Barbie's..

A Very Important Visit

Throughout the years, my family and I have tried to share our bounty at Christmas with people who need more than they have. We've gotten ideas from the priests at the church and those ideas sent us on exciting missions with teens and others in groups or schools.

As our grandson got old enough to participate, we took him with us to the grocery store to help select the food for the boxes we would take to our adopted families. Before his first visit we explained that we needed to stretch the dollars we had to spend as far as possible to provide as many meals as we could. We explained that the family we had been given by the agency was larger than our own and each meal required a lot more food. We explained that we believed that as the agency screened families in need, that God chose the family assigned for us.

As we walked the aisles we had to remind him that this family was Hispanic and would not like eating some foods he liked so we went to buy rice and beans. He lifted the big bags from the bottom shelves and was very happy. Sometimes we bought a store gift coupon for the meat, but this time we had called ahead and were bringing the whole meal with us.

Our daughter, Stefanie, called specifically to ask if they had an oven. Unfortunately her college Spanish vocabulary did not stretch to "oven" and the lady on the phone spoke no English.

Undaunted Stefanie continued to ask about cooking a turkey. The word she used was not correct, the lady explained. Stefanie tried again to communicate. "Can you cook a grande, grande pollo?" she asked. The lady laughed and said she could. By then Stefanie was laughing, too. She had asked if they could cook a big, big, chicken!

We found a ham on sale, bought the turkey and a big roast beef visualizing beef tacos, burros and enchiladas. But Johnathan was not satisfied. He went down the aisle and picked up 3 boxes of cake mix and some frosting. Then he put a huge liter bottle of soft drink into the cart. In spite of the boxes of candy canes we would include, in his view, the children needed dessert and treats.

That afternoon I joined my family in the Santa suit to make the delivery of the specific gifts each child had requested and the many bags of food. I had stuffed animals, candy canes, and some of the specific gifts they had requested in my velvet bag along with a trunk full of food and gifts.

Stefanie remembers that all that food represented only a little more than our family of four buys each week.

I thought I was familiar with the streets of Phoenix, but I was quite surprised when we finally found the part of the street with our family's address. It was a dirt road! It was not in the country either. It was by the airport in the center of the city.

We noticed the cracked sidewalk and the broken steps to the house, but we also noticed that the dirt yard had been swept. We knocked on the door and I waited. A little boy of about 5 years old came running from around the corner of the house with an excited face. "I speak English!", he said.

We asked for his mother and sisters and brothers. "In the bathtub", he said matter of factly.

I thought that was a little strange since we had arranged the time for our visit carefully. He showed us inside and the five of us filled the tiny living room. He had thought ahead, however, and ushered me to a big chair in a corner and invited me to sit down.

In a few minutes, mother, 2 sisters, 3 brothers all came out still a little damp, but very excited. There was also an aunt and many cousins. They loved seeing Santa. Most of the children spoke English and enjoyed talking to me. The mother and the aunt were looking at the kitchen, however. That was my clue to suggest we see what else was in the car.

As I opened the trunk, children from up and down the street came to watch. One little neighbor boy asked, "Is all that food for one family?" I have never forgotten his plaintiff question. I often wonder if he had Christmas dinner, or any dinner at all.

Our adopted family was thrilled with the food. The mother laughed with Stefanie when they brought in the grande, grande, pollo. The aunt helped put the food away and the meat stuffed their tiny refrigerator.

Everyone went back into the living room where I was sitting with the children. They had more to tell me and wanted to show me each gift they had unwrapped. Then it was time to go.

That is when I noticed that my bag which had been sitting on the floor beside me all this time, was dripping wet. Water actually dropped off of it. I didn't know what to do at first. Then I just made sure I carried it in front of me away from my velvet suit all the way to the car. At the car I enlisted the aid of my family to help with the wet bag, animals and candy.

We had to race home because I was already late for my next engagement. Now I had to restock a new, dry bag with animals and hurry out.

The animals on the bottom two layers of the bag were ruined. You see, stuffed animals never dry completely without molding. As we drove and worked with the wet bag we kept wondering how it had gotten so wet.

Then it occurred to us. The family God had given to us had worked hard to make their home perfect for our visit. They cleaned, swept the dirt yard**, and washed the carpet.**

Unfortunately, they did not have a machine to extract the water after the washing and it remained a wet, but clean, area for my bag.

Many people have looked forward to my visits. Many have spent a lot of time preparing for the event, but I remember how completely dedicated that family was to making sure to present their very best to Santa. In halting Spanish and mostly English I had told them the story of Jesus' coming at Christmas. I pointed to the picture of Jesus on their wall and their faces beamed. They had prepared their home for the coming of our Lord as well.

International Santa

Over the years Santa has had a lot of names such as, Father Christmas and Kinter Claus. In some countries the stories say he dresses all in fur. But for many people, there is no Santa Claus; no gifts; no special food and candy.

I have visited people in the United States who have made their home here after struggling to emigrate from many lands. We have friends from China who loved to give me Mexican food. Our holiday celebrations with them still bring joy to my heart. We have Mexican friends who bring us tamales or give us a free meal in their Mexican restaurant.

For 15 years we have known a lot of people from Africa. Some have come here to study and we have enjoyed helping them understand the joys of American ways of life, especially Santa's gifts. In recent years we have deliberately met and come to love nearly 40 "Lost Boys" of the Sudan who have come to Phoenix to live. They had never heard of Santa Claus or the North Pole. I had to be careful when I told them the story of Santa delivering presents to children everywhere in just one night because no Santa had ever delivered any gifts to them even at Christmas! They had watched their friends die in great numbers. They blessed God for food to eat. They built their own structures out of mud after they had walked 1000 miles.

They knew me well from all the time we had spent together at doctors' offices, arranging classes, job interviews, and church so when I went to visit them wearing the red velvet suit, they laughed. After some explanation and a bit of explanation from TV commercials, these Sudanese refugees came to understand the spirit of Santa. You see, they already understood the real meaning of Christmas was Jesus' birth. We just introduced them to gifts. Lost Boys have their own story.

I've met refugees from Afghanistan, Somalia, Kenya, Congo and Uganda. These people may not respond to stories of Jesus because they are Muslim, but they do respond with smiles to the love Santa brings and the gifts of candy.

It was intentional when we invited our friends from Germany to stay in our home during one Christmas. They were open-mouthed at the extent of what one Santa Claus can do in the few days they were with us. Their traditions are different in so many ways from ours, but essentially we all have experienced the love and gift giving from our cultural experience and out of bounty.

Last weekend, however, was a surprise. I had been invited to attend a party at the home of a new friend. We had only met him and he just asked me to stop by to visit his workers who I knew were mostly Mexican.

I had visited enough kids living in the barrios of Phoenix that I had intentionally learned a bit of Spanish to talk to them. I always hope Mexican adults know English because I have never studied Spanish. I knew I would be fine when the children asked for toys, however, because Barbie and Nintendo are the same in ANY language!

The party was going well when I arrived and the children loved Santa. Then I met my new friend's wife. She is from Hungary. Her parents are from Austria and Czechlosvakia. They went across the street to get their neighbors from Russia.

Santa may dress in different costumes around the world. He may have unique names or be totally unknown in some cultures. But in America, this Santa at least, has met people from all around the world and brought joy and Jesus' love through a tiny stuffed animal, a big smile and a candy cane without leaving home.

Treasures From the Heart

People are kind and basically good, especially children. A great number of people want to offer to give something to me because they have been touched by something I said or a memory of a happy time Santa's love or gift brought to their mind. They offer from a sense of generosity and usually from their abundance.

Financial gifts keep this ministry funded for candy canes and animals. I am grateful for generosity and abundance.

I am also grateful for the generous hearts of the children who make certain that Santa shares their bounty at parties. They toddle over and offer me a lick of their sticky candy canes.

Last week I was at a party that had been beautifully catered with elegant food and beautiful desserts. Whole families had come and enjoyed shrimp and truffles. One entire table near the Christmas Tree was stacked with a tower of Gingerbread Men. They looked like the real one that ran all over town in the story.

One little girl thought they tasted good, too. She was about 4 years old and she carried one in each hand.

After she would eat part of it, she would come back to see me and offer me the other half of the cookie. I can't accept food from the children for a lot of reasons, but she was undaunted and continued to bring me half cookies all evening. I was touched by her generosity.

Yesterday it was a little hard to be grateful for the Christmas cards lovingly made by little hands at the school for disadvantaged children. Their classrooms had been chosen by the counselors as needing a lot of help with Christmas. High school classes had bought gifts and made food and taken a party to these younger children. I was part of the party!

One of the activities the little children could do during their free afternoon was to make beautiful cards that said, "SANTA" in multicolored glitter and a LOT of glue. These little ones worked diligently and brought their offerings to me with great happiness and pride. I accepted them with thanks intending to carry them carefully away from my velvet and let them dry in the car.

Helpfully, someone placed all the gluey cards and a big piece of soft chocolate into my velvet bag with a lot of candy canes. I discovered the problem when I went into the school office to greet the principal and pulled out a glittery, chocolate smeared candy cane.

It will take a miracle to clean the bag, but everyone helped and I left behind a lot of glittery candy for someone to clean off for the rest of the school.

Remember that I understand how it feels to want to share your own joy with someone else. I get to do it all of December and often the rest of the year. I am grateful for what they give, but one gift I got this year will always have a special place in my heart.

I was at a church party given for homeless or indigent, possibly undocumented, Mexican families. They had a huge meal with a lot of tamales, music, and a pile of gifts for Santa to give to each one.

One little boy, about 5 years old, was especially thrilled with Santa Claus. He stared and stood close by my chair. He spent so much time there, that I began to let him help me search my bag for little stuffed reindeer and candy canes.

At last, the food was eaten and the gifts were given out. It was time to pack up to go home. My new little friend looked very somber and then he smiled a gorgeous big smile. He stuck his hand deep down into his pocket and pulled something out.

He came up to my lap and stretched out his hand offering me something in his hand. I reached out to accept his offering and with his smile getting even bigger, he handed me a blue plastic lid.   It was typical of a little boy to have a pocket with strange items in it.

What was not typical, however, is that this little boy had no home. He had nothing to call his own except his blue plastic lid. He was so excited to give it to me and I was so touched to receive it. I have it in a special place in my home. I suspect it will live later in my own treasure box.

He reminded me of Jesus' parable of the widow's mite. Many have much more to give. But Jesus taught that God gives great value to the mite of the widow who had nothing. From one who has nearly nothing, even a tiny offering is all he had to give.

Thank you, Manuel

Unsuspecting, Santa's Helpers

I pressed the button on the remote control to open the garage door. It was nearly nine in the evening and I was looking forward to whatever supper my wife had been able to save for a tired Santa Claus. Lunch seemed far behind me now and stretching in front of me was the large task of loading my van to the roof with animals and candy canes for seeing the large groups of boys and girls scheduled for the next day.

The mountain of brown cartons in the garage left barely enough room for the van to back up to the garage under the roof. I stepped out ahead of the rain that was threatening to begin at any moment. The sound of the opening garage door and the jingling bells on my Santa boots alerted my wife that I was at home.

She was smiling when I looked at her. There was a mysterious white dusty powder on the floor of the garage and on some of the boxes of stuffed animals. "What's that?" I questioned. "Oh, how are you tonight?"

It was a few seconds before she solved the riddle of the white powder I had scraped into a little pile on top of a box of green frogs. "Gear dust" she said "just another little miracle wrought by Santa's helpers while you were gone."

"Not again", I thought. "Always in December. What happened?"

Late on Friday afternoon, my wife had tried to open the garage door with the automatic opener. When it refused to go up, she checked the electricity and realized that the fault lay in the opening unit. With one minute to go, she called the company that had installed and repaired that door before.

"Sorry, lady. Everybody's gone home for the weekend. We do have an emergency service, though. Maybe he'll answer and maybe he'll come out in the rain that'll be here soon. That'll be an extra $50. Payable when he gets there."

"Do you want me to call him?"

"Yes," she whispered. "Yes." I knew she was worried about how to pay for the unexpected expense and emergency fee. December was a month with no income in her business and none for this volunteer Santa either.

She also knew, however, that after lifting several thousand children onto my knee in the past weeks that my back was sore. It would be hard enough to load the boxes of animals and candy into the van tonight with an open garage door. If it wouldn't go up, I would have to unload each box, carry small bags of animals through the whole house and walk through the yard in the rain to the van. I hated to think how long that would have taken for a man as tired and hungry as I was then.

I gave her a hug with which I meant to say, "I love you," "Thank you". "Don't be afraid" all at once.

Two Decembers later, there was a huge "thwack" sound like an explosion, my family said. They investigated in the garage and found that the huge apring around the garage door was in two pieces and the door would not move! It wouldn't even move with the manual override.

The garage was filled again with boxes and boxes of candy canes and stuffed animals. Santa was out in the rain and expected in just an hour to return to reload the car and make another appearance where people were expecting him to help make their Christmas celebration.

My wife called the garage door service again. "It is December again. Santa's toys are in the garage and the big spring is broken! Can you help us right away?"

The young man who answered did not remember the last event, but his boss remembered fixing Santa's garage. "He has to get thousands of toys out of the garage this weekend" he said to the young man. "We'll have to find someone to get right out there."

My wife was reassured. When the repairmen arrived...there were three this time, they made short work of fixing the garage. I arrived in time to see them putting the final touches on the job and starting to write the bill for overtime again.

When they saw that I was really Santa, they reduced their fee to the normal repair price. I was able to give them toys for their children so that they could say to them, "Daddy got this from the hand of Santa himself just for you."

Santa's helpers. God's angels. It takes a lot of help to remind people of the Reason for the Season...Jesus' Birth.

RATS

"Rats!" The words sputtered out of my mouth again, "Rats?"

Tears began to glisten in the brown eyes of the 5-year-old girl on my knee. I had just asked her what she wanted Santa to bring her for Christmas that year when she stated with firmness and confidence, "Rats".

"Well, Darla," I managed at last, reading her name tag and managing to smile with my lips at least, "Santa always tries to bring the things children tell him they want the most. But I have to admit, no one has ever asked me for rats before."

I lifted my eyes and searched the room for help. Instead of help, I saw the executive director with her mouth wide open in shock. There was one woman who was beginning to come forward to see Darla and I, but she wasn't smiling helpfully either.

Around the festive hall were whole families having fun, eating dessert, waiting for their turn to visit with Santa. Each family had one thing in common—at least one of their children had hemophilia, the disorder of blood that has no clotting factor. Children born with the disease do not have an easy life. Their lives are filled with pain, doctors, emergency rooms and frequent injections.

Even with great medical advances of this century they face frozen joints, death from minor accidents and even AIDS from a contaminated blood supply that provides the clotting factor injections each one must have to live.

The Hemophilia Association provides medical information and assistance to the families affected. Usually it is serious business of life and pain, but for tonight, the association had sponsored the annual Christmas party where all the families could be together with only a happy agenda. I had attended their parties as Santa for many years and always fell totally in love with the children who came to see me.

Tonight Darla and I were sharing a serious moment — alone.

"Darla, I have given away thousands of stuffed bears, raccoons, koalas, monkeys, bunnies and lambs. Would you like something like that?" I pleaded.

"No, Santa. It has to be rats." She was serious, and firm. Her head nodded slowly up and down and her eyes never left mine.

"My brother has hemophilia" she explained. "No one knows much about how to stop it or cure it. My mommy told me that doctors try to invent some medicine to make my brother better, but they can't give it to people right away in case it isn't good for them. So, the doctors give the new medicine to rats first."
She waited for me to understand. I must not have looked convinced because she continued.

"Rats! Santa. The doctors need many more rats so they can work faster to get a new medicine to fix my brother."

Now it was my eyes that had glistening tears and I couldn't speak for a minute. I did smile for Darla and finally I was able to say, "Sweet girl, Santa will bring many rats this Christmas. Thank you for being so filled with love."

People have asked for cars, husbands, babies, money, movie stars, vacations, jobs, and many other things, but the greatest, most unselfish request this Santa ever had was for rats.

Jenny's Friend

Jenny was a beautiful bride. She had always been beautiful and a special friend and helper for Santa. As a young girl she was an acolyte at the church and Santa John, the lay reader, helped her whenever she was uncertain just what she was supposed to be doing. After her father died, she really seemed to feel close to John.

Long after she was in college, she still came to the children's service on Christmas Eve to help give the candy canes to Santa who was busy with children crowded around him for 350 degrees. Jenny was part of our church life and now she was a married woman.

The setting was lovely, outside in the dusk with purple views of the desert and mountains in the distance. It was still hot, however. Too hot to move around much so we sat at a table to watch the younger crowd moving and celebrating.

Another beautiful young woman came to sit at our tiny table. She introduced herself to us and we all reminisced about how we had known Jenny. I mentioned that I had held her on my knee when she was just a little girl.

"I have been thinking that you look like Santa," she exclaimed with great excitement. She told me that she had always loved Christmas and its celebration of Christ's birth, but especially she had loved Santa Claus.
After about an hour, I asked her about the lovely scarf she wore on her head and she told me she had a brain tumor and had lost her hair from the treatments. She told me about the Brain Tumor Support Group she attends at a local hospital.

"Would you be willing to come to our Christmas party this year?" she asked. "Everyone would be so excited. It is an upbeat group of people and families who come to the Christmas party. Sometimes there are kids, too. It would be so much fun. Would you mind? Can you come? I'll call you. I'll come to get you? You don't have to bring presents."

I could only smile as she continued to talk. When she stopped to breathe, I agreed to come to the party for her new friends.

Francis did call and Santa went to the party at the hospital for those surviving with brain tumors. They were a happy group and really did enjoy seeing Santa for 3 years with Francis.

One November she didn't call, but her friends did. They were having an early Christmas celebration with Francis in the nursing home where she had had to move. Would I come? She always loved Santa so much.

Of course I went with bells and candy and a present for her. She was talking to me and so happy to have all her family and friends gathered together for a special Christmas before she died. I continue to visit the Christmas Party for the Brain Tumor Support Group. We all remember Francis and how much she loved to celebrate the season.

That would have been the end of the story that year, but the next Thanksgiving week I received a call from a man who said, "Santa, you don't know me, but I am Francis's brother. You saw my children at her early Christmas party last year and they were very excited. Last weekend they asked me when they were going to see the REAL SANTA again. Upon questioning, I realized they were talking about you."

It seems he had spent 4 days tracking down how to call me because his children wanted to see the REAL SANTA again. He said, "I told them that sometimes something like that happens only once in a lifetime. Seeing the REAL SANTA is a very special event."

His request wasn't just for his own children, however. He wanted me to visit his whole cub scout troop for their party because he thought those other little boys should have a chance to see the REAL SANTA while they still believe.

God rest you, Merry, Francis. I believe they celebrate Christmas in Heaven. If they didn't before, I'll bet they do now.

CHANUKAH SANTA?

The pharmacist opened a new camera to take pictures of his staff and patients when Santa went in to visit. Everyone was so excited to see Santa that it warmed his heart. When I asked him to come to sit on my knee, he shook his head and faded behind others who were eager to come forward.

David wasn't usually so shy about things. I wondered why he was reticent to come today. Then I realized! He is Jewish! He doesn't think it would be right for him to sit on my knee because he knows I am a Christian Santa helping celebrate the birth of Jesus.

"Come on up here, David," I said. "Come on. Santa loves you. I am sure there is something in this bag for good little Jewish boys, too."

Everyone laughed, especially David. He broke into a huge grin and came to sit on my lap at last. I doubt anyone else enjoyed his little raccoon that afternoon as much as he did. He said, "My boys always wanted to see Santa. Now I know why!"

"I can come to see them if you wouldn't mind" I offered. "Oh, Santa, we are having a huge party this weekend for Chanukah. Would you come and be our Chanukah Santa?"

Everyone laughed, but I agreed and got directions to his home. How could I refuse a man who had saved the lives of 3 of my family catching pharmaceutical errors in prescriptions? I went expectantly. What an exciting afternoon with so many children who had never seen Santa up close. It was pretty exciting to learn that a lot of the parents had not seen Santa before either.

I went about spreading cheer, delivering a few stuffed animals to people who looked a little depressed and candy canes to everyone. No one asked me to tell him the Christmas story. I wasn't surprised, but I was pleased at how happy everyone there was to see Santa. It was the same response I saw at other parties where people see Santa and perk up with smiles and joy. Everyone had a good time.

When I got home, I remembered how much my next-door neighbor loved seeing me come and go in the costume. For several years he would make a point of stepping into his driveway to watch me pull away with a load of toys. He would wave and smile and say, "I knew it was that time of year when I heard your bells." I am sure it was noisy as I loaded my car taking trip after trip from the garage with bells jingling on the boots. I have learned it is impossible for this Santa to be secretive or to sneak up on anyone while in the costume.

He was a judge and could wear the most perfect stern face worthy of the bench. I usually saw his smile, however, whenever he saw Santa.

Today I was thinking of him especially after the Chanukah party. I knocked on their door when I got home invited them to come next door to our house where I knew we had a camera with film.

"Sit on Santa's lap" I invited and he sat with great joy to receive his little bear. Someone snapped his picture and his wife said, "I believe that is the first picture you have ever had on Santa's knee. What will your friends at temple say?"

In just a few minutes, I invited her to come to sit on my lap, but she was very reluctant to do so. She had never been to see Santa before. Somehow, I was real to her. I represented the celebration of Christmas. I was no longer just John in the red suit. I reminded her that we had celebrated Passover with them in their home and I wanted her to experience a little time on Santa's knee. Then I promised never to tell her family, especially her mother.

She sat and had her picture taken and enjoyed her bear. I learned that many Jewish people enjoy the love and joy expressed at Christmas, especially by Santa.

Postscript: Our neighbor continued to live next door even after her husband had died. There is another story about her. It happened almost 20 years later. She had been making donations to North Pole Ministries for many years. Our God is good.

Do You Have 2000 Moose?

The semi truck driver was nervous about being parked in a residential neighborhood. "They should have sent another truck" he said. "I'm not sure I am in the right place."

"You are if you have 2000 stuffed moose" my wife answered.

"I don't know what's in those boxes, but I'll just drop them in the street". He was walking quickly to the truck.

"Please wait" my wife called. "It is going to rain and I can't lift a pallet of boxes into the garage alone!" "Do you have a pallet mover?"

"I have one, Madam, but I don't have time to use it here. I'll get a ticket."

"I'll promise no ticket if you'll move those 2000 moose into my garage for Santa Claus", she said.

He wasn't sure, but agreed to let her look at the boxes before he slid them to the tailgate. "Wooly Moose" the boxes read. "These are perfect", she exclaimed.

Reluctantly the driver lowered the tailgate and the pallet mover to the street level. Then he began to move the first pallet up the driveway.

My wife ran ahead to open the garage door for him. I drove up just then in my Santa suit to reload the car with animals and candy enroute to the next Christmas event.

"Santa", she called "this man is worried about getting a ticket for parking his big truck here, but he is unloading the moose anyway."

I caught her hint and went up to him immediately with candy canes and a stuffed animal. After a while, his frown softened a bit until after the last load with the pallet carrier, he smiled back at me.

I asked if he had children and as he was telling me about his family, he told me about his brother from Texas who had come here to live and die with them.

"I would be happy to go to see him if you think Santa will make him happy", I offered.

"No, Santa, I'll just take him this little animal, if that's all right" he said. "We're just a poor black family and I know you'll be too busy for us."

"If he only knew that 90% of my time and animals go to poor families and they will get these 2000 wooly moose, too," I thought.

Eventually I was able to get his phone number and we arranged a time for me to come to visit Garvin.

I knew I had the right street, but there were no house numbers on any homes in the cul de sac. There were about 12 neighborhood teens standing in the street, however, so I asked if they knew where Garvin's address was located.

"Why?" one asked. There was silence and no information.

So I responded, "I am here to visit him and hope to make him feel a little better. He is very sick." Now there were a few smiles and less threatening postures when they pointed to the right house.

Almost before I got to the door, there were neighborhood children surrounding me. Parents and others were being alerted to Santa's visit all over the neighborhood by the "group" of boys guarding the street. The house was full and overflowing with neighbors and kids. Everyone had a good time. They took pictures. They sang.

Garvin had a wonderful time during our visit and then Garvin asked me to pray for him.

I prayed for Garvin to be healed and for all those who love him. The family prayed and the neighbors prayed. It was a memorable evening for each of us. I hope it was for the children and teens of that neighborhood, too.

I'll never forget Garvin or his brother who brought the 2000 wooly moose that have their own story.

Chet

As you might expect, I need to know the newest toys and electronic wishes of my young visitors. When they sit on my lap and ask for something I've never heard of before, it hurts their level of confidence and belief in the Santa that makes all toys. I study the toy catalogues, I visit toy stores and I interview older children to ask their guesses about what the little kids will want.

For the same reasons I went to see the movie, "The Santa Clause", with Tim Allen. I knew the children would have seen it and I needed to know what they were thinking. By the time "Santa Clause II" was released, I was happy to go having enjoyed the first one and Tim Allen a lot. I particularly enjoyed watching the reindeer in training in the second movie slip and slide his way throughout the movie. Poor Chet never did get it just right even at the end while pulling the sleigh on Christmas Eve.

That year the toy budget was small and I wanted to be prepared for the growing number of Boys and Girls Clubs that asked me to serve as their Santa. Each one had 400-800 kids and each child needed to have a stuffed toy and a candy cane.

I found a closeout catalogue from an advertising specialty manufacturer offering 6" stuffed moose for $1.00. The company had 2000 in stock, "naked". ("Naked" refers to the fact that they are not wearing shirts or hats or scarves with company logos or advertising which would be normal in the ad specialty business.)

I always try to provide good quality animals because these children often get no other gift for Christmas. For the same reason, I will not give away stuffed mice or rats no matter how "cute" they may be, even if they are free. These kids live with vermin and would not think rats to be cute no matter how they are clothed.

I ordered the entire stock of naked wooly moose and waited for them to be delivered. I waited and waited and worried after I got the invoice for only 6 boxes. "Those must be huge boxes", I thought.

The day the moose were delivered I opened the first box immediately and could hardly contain my disappointment. My wife and daughter were there and each was despondent thinking about how puny and scrawny these moose looked. 6" is tall enough for a nice animal, but these were only a few inches wide…skinny! Not impressive.

While we were discussing what to do about the disappointed children who would be at the Boys and Girls Clubs, our young Grandson came running outside.
 His mother said, "What do you think of these reindeer, Johnathan?" (We always knew we would call them reindeer because they had antlers. What else would Santa give?)

"OH, CHET" he said with a big smile.

So that is how one scrawny wooly moose became the most popular animal toy I ever gave to children. Somehow God and the magic of the fur trimmed, red velvet Santa bag transformed those disappointing moose into the beloved reindeer Chet.

2000 kids smiled at me as I handed them their moose. "Oh, Chet" they understood.

God's miracles extend to stuffed toys and the hearts of children.

The Most Unusual Santa Visit

For the 37 years of being Santa I have made sure to visit the cemetery in costume to take a stuffed animal and a candy cane heart to the grave of one special child, my son Sean.

Sean died before I ever wore the costume, when my only experience as Santa was on Christmas Eve at midnight putting together the pedal car that came without 3 essential bolts & nuts.

This year I stopped by on a sunny afternoon and noted how nice the grass looked this winter. The cemetery had grown so much since we had been coming there, but grave stones here are still flat in the ground to accommodate year round mowing.

I put the little animal in the space for the flower vase and arranged the candy canes into the shape of a heart. As I was saying my prayers and thanking God for our son, a woman walked up and touched me.

She asked me if I would come with her to a grave across the street for just a little while. She pointed and I agreed to meet her there when I was finished with my prayers.

My car was fully loaded with toys so I drove around the circular drive closer to where the lady was standing.

  After parking, I walked over to her carrying my usual offering of candy canes and stuffed animals.

"Thank you so much for coming with me to my daughter's grave," she said. "She died before we ever took her to see Santa Claus and have her picture taken. I don't know why we didn't go in those six years, but she was sick and we were busy, I guess. We have missed her so much in these 2 months since she died, but Christmas is going to be even harder without her. Somehow I believe that if I could look at her picture with Santa and remember how happy she was that I would feel better."

"Would you let me take your picture here, with her headstone for her first visit with Santa?"

I arranged the candy canes into a heart on the headstone and placed a little stuffed animal beside it and knelt down so that she could get a perfect picture of Santa Claus and her daughter's name.

Tears were flowing down her cheeks when I got up. I gave her a big hug, a small animal and showed her how the two candy canes will make a heart to forever remind her she is never alone, but loved by God.

"Thank you" she called to me as I walked to my car.
"Thank you, God" I prayed "for the gift of our children here and in Heaven".

"Everyone" Loves Santa

Over the years of our marriage my wife and I have adopted a special project or family every Christmas. Some years our gift was more time than monetary, but we have been consistent in trying to bring joy to the hearts of someone outside our family during the blessed season.

As a salesman I have been in so many businessmen's offices, seen so many manufacturers, wholesalers, finishers and shippers who employ thousands of people. Some have Christmas parties for their staff, some give them gifts, but occasionally a business owner would ask me what they could do to help someone outside their own shop. It has always been a thrill to help them find someone who needs their help.

The story of one such business is interesting because no one in the entire company had ever adopted a family at Christmas. They did not have any idea what to do to begin such a project. They only knew that it sounded like a good idea and they knew they wanted to be personally involved in the process.

I helped the company owners find an agency to give them a family who needed help. We knew the family had been screened and the employees would not be disappointed that their hard work might go to someone who had money in the bank.

I helped them make lists of food items they thought this Hispanic family might enjoy. We had lists of clothing sizes and toy "wishes" of the children. The ladies who worked in this laboratory and office based business looked forward to the shopping. The men volunteered to get the truck they would need to haul the items to the family.

"Santa, will you come with us on December 22 at 4 PM when we are going to deliver our food and toys to our family? None of us knows what to do. We aren't sure what to say. We don't speak Spanish. Do you?"

"Not but a few essential words", I said, "but the kids will understand that you are bringing gifts and who I am. Actually it will probably be the children who translate our English to their parents."

When their flat bed truck parked in front of the adopted family's home, I could hardly believe my eyes. They had 50 pound bags of beans and rice and flour, cases of tomatoes and chilies, and bags of dried spices and chili peppers. There was a car load of wrapped gifts and 3 bikes strapped to the cab of the truck. Clearly, the employees had gotten into the spirit of giving that year.

The children raced across the flooded yard bouncing on the boards that stretched from the sidewalk to the front stoop and splashing mud as they came.

I thought of my red velvet and took slow careful steps alone when it came to be my turn to cross the mud and flood.

Everyone in that household was happy. The children were excited to see Santa, but almost as excited to see the food. The adults saw gifts for the kids and the bikes. The father peeked his head in for a minute and smiled at the stacks of food he saw. Everyone from my customer's business was excited and happy at the joy they had brought to that home.

The business owners and their employees left soon after the trucks were empty. I stayed until all the children and their friends had had a chance to talk to Santa. When I stood up to leave, the whole family was there to hug me one last time and to wave goodbye.

I was hardly able to see the boards clearly in the waning daylight, but I made it across the yard safely and then I couldn't find my car keys!

I knew I hadn't taken them out inside the house. I didn't want to try to get back across the muddy yard in the dark. I searched my bag and then began to empty it out onto the trunk of the car. By then I was very aware that about 10 surly gang guys had gathered on the corner nearby. They were calling out to each other about the white guy in the Mercedes.

I kept on looking for the keys and racking my brain for where they could have been dropped.

By now my Santa bag was empty and there were stuffed animals all over my car trunk. There were now about 15 gang guys all around me and my car, too.

"Merry Christmas" I said to them smiling brightly in the dark. "How are you tonight?" I kept on thinking.

"Would you like to have this candy cane?" I asked the guy nearest me. He took it and actually smiled. When he did, the others moved closer and I began handing candy to each one. Pretty soon they began taking the stuffed animals off of the trunk. When they were gone, others were asking for more.

"If you can help me find my car keys," I said, "I'll be able to give you more animals I have here in the trunk." They produced a light and looked on the ground and all along the muddy walk. I shook my bag one more time and heard something hit the ground.

MY KEYS! "Here come more animals" I exclaimed as I opened the trunk. By then the gang guys had brought their brothers and sisters out from their houses to see Santa. I guess there were 50 or more kids all around me. I know I gave away every single animal I had and all the candy, too.

As I got into the car I could see another sinister looking group of guys on the next corner.

The guys around me saw them, too, and said to me, "We'll stay with you until you are out of the neighborhood. Don't drive too fast now. Some will follow you and some will walk ahead and you'll be just fine."

I left waving and shouting, "Merry Christmas". They waved and smiled too.

No matter who you are or how tough your life makes you be, you can relax and enjoy the spirit of giving and love at Christmas. May God grant happiness and peace to the households Santa touched that night.

Children at Any Age

For over twenty years, I have been privileged to be the official Santa at the Christmas party given for residents of a home for developmentally challenged adults. These children at heart react and interact with me as though they were just five years old.

When I go into their party they have finished dinner and often a program or pageant about the Christmas story. Someone provides a nice gift for each resident of the homes and I bring a stuffed animal and a candy cane. Each resident comes to sit on Santa's lap and asks for something they really want.

One year every single resident wanted headphones. I was not surprised to learn that new rules were to begin the following week for the good of everyone living in the group setting. From that time forward music had to be heard through headphones only to protect the hearing of others and avoid fussing over what was playing.

These adults with developmental disabilities still know a lot of things from TV and movies. After they saw the Santa Claus movies they always asked me questions about the workshop and North Pole. One year a resident really wanted a cell phone. I asked him if he knew how to buy one and he admitted that he did not even know where to shop.

I said for all his friends from the home to hear, "Then let's call Bernard and ask him to put a cell phone on your list." They were all very excited to see his face when "Bernard" answered my red cell phone and talked to him. They left the party that year certain that he had ordered his gift directly from the head elf.

Some years they are like other groups of kids and want all kinds of things. They want a big screen TV, or a pick up truck. Two of them want to get married. But this year each of the women wanted a baby! That involved a discussion that was not my place to have in front of a room full of people. What was I to do?

Thankfully they are easily distracted so I asked, "What did you have for dinner"?
"Chicken" was the reply.
"Did you save me any?" I asked.
Looking bewildered, she said finally, "No".
Did you save me dessert?" I asked.
"NO," she answered, then her face brightened, "but I know where the kitchen is".

Sometimes individuals or organizations donate a collection of new stuffed animals for Santa to give to children at Christmas. Usually we buy a large number of toys all the same size so that no disparity is perceived by the myriad of children who might receive one. Collections can cause a problem, however. Often they are many sizes and *size* is what matters.

Children don't notice the more expensive animals with joints that move or ones that have expensive clothing with petticoats and hats. They just notice that Santa gave another child a toy BIGGER than his own. Last year a large public charity gave us 50 HUGE stuffed animals. They were all kinds of animals and all colors. They took up a large part of the garage and Santa needed to find them a home.

As I was marking each shipping box with the name of the charity group where I would take those specific animals, I came to the 10 boxes of these huge animals and stopped, stumped.

My wife is the one who mentioned that there were exactly the numbers of huge animals as these "kids" from the home. Perfect!, I thought, but the home director is very strict about what items they can have in their rooms. Space is at a premium there so I decided to call him to warn about the size of the gift. He was decidedly apprehensive, but then turned a positive light on it…"We'll have a grand cleanout the week before the party so everyone will have room for the toy Santa will bring. Yes. That will work out perfectly."

You cannot imagine the joy in the eyes of each of those residents as they received their own stuffed animal bigger and fatter than a king sized pillow. The animals were so big that extra cars had to be added to the caravan of volunteer drivers that take them home after the party.

These residents may function at about age 5 or 9 years, but they are actually as old as 77 years. One woman has been a resident there for 47 years. They have had joint replacements, cancer, cataracts, dentures and other maladies common to those who are aging. Most have no close family because their parents have died leaving them in a loving home that is run by volunteers and paid staff.

They go to church, camp, parties and sometimes sheltered workshops. They love to prepare for the Christmas party. They begin learning their song in June. Some take part in a pageant.

One year a man was still wearing part of a costume when he came to sit on Santa's lap so I asked him, "What are you?"

"I'm a wise man" he said.
"Which one", I asked.
His look was as blank as it could be. He had no idea! I called on their Sunday school teacher to help him. "Which wise man is he?" I asked.

Another blank look. By now the volunteers, class members, church members, families, staff and friends are all smiling and laughing.   No one is calling out suggestions, though.

"Are you sure that you cannot remember the wise men's names?" I asked the Sunday School teacher. He was embarrassed by now and everyone was really laughing.

None of the 30+ friends was offering any help, either. He was shaking his head by now so I said to the whole group, "Does anyone know the names of the wise men who followed the star to Bethlehem to worship the baby Jesus?"

Finally I began to hear suggestions from around the crowded room. They weren't always right, so before I left I told everyone the names of the three: Balthazar, Gaspar, and Melchior.

As I gave a little hug to the man on my lap and turned to leave, I said to everyone "I'll be back next year. I hope you'll all remember the names of the wise men until then."

They don't remember from year to year, but each year I ask and each year now they turn to their teacher in preparation for his attempt to name the wise men. He usually gets two right.

These kids and their teacher may not remember the details of the Christmas story, but they know its essence. They know that God sent His Son Jesus as the greatest gift the world has ever seen. In their child like faith, they "know" and "believe". The facts are not important.

"Whoever receives this little child in My name receives Me; and whoever receives Me receives Him who sent Me" Luke 10: 48

Santa Sees The Forgotten

I visit a lot of people in hospitals. Their family or their friends think they will be cheered up by a hospital visit from Santa Claus. Usually they are right. When I come in patients have a few minutes when they can think about something other than their pain and live a little in the happy memories of other, better Christmases.

As soon as I have seen the patient for whom I received a visit request, there is always a nurse waiting there asking me to visit just one more patient with her. The nurses know who needs a bit of cheer. They know who doesn't have visitors or family support. I am happy to go with them and I have been in some amazing situations as a result of these impromptu visits.

As I said, the nurse is always thinking of a patient who needs a visit. I don't leave the floor, however, until I have held each nurse and aide on my lap and given them a little animal and a candy cane. They may not be the poor or the weak of our world, but they are the givers and are rarely recognized. They find a camera or a cell phone and take pictures of each other and any doctor who walks by. On Santa's knee they can be like kids and accept something for themselves for a few minutes.

I learned how much medical nurses needed appreciation in hospitals, so I decided to try to visit all our family's doctors and their staff during December. As Santa and his family have aged, there are more and more places to visit.

The doctors are fascinated that Santa has come and enjoy the smiles and excitement of their staff. The girls and guys who work in all the capacities of medical support have a good time making sure that everyone has their picture taken on Santa's knee. I usually see the little animals I give them still at their workstations throughout the year.

They tell me that no other patients give them gifts. Some send postcards from trips and a few holiday cards, but only drug reps and Santa give gifts. The motives are decidedly different.

One of my daughter's new doctors was so excited that I had come to see him, that he called her to thank her. He even sent a donation to the charity. While I was in his office he and his staff had a good time taking pictures. Then he led me into a room filled with people in recliner chairs. They were all getting chemotherapy! You can imagine how bad they were feeling just then, but the bells on my shoes, the stuffed animals and candy cane brought smiles to all their faces. That is a trip I will always repeat! In fact I now visit several chemotherapy rooms, each several times a season because of the tremendous joyful impact my
visit has on the patients and the staff. The doctors go out of their way to impress on me how all the members of their staff are uplifted by the fact that Santa has come to see their sickest patients. Nurses usually see them in pain and suffering, but after my visit they say there are smiles all around and the joy carries on for several days.

After several years living in the desert, Santa developed allergies. Because I am in the Santa suit from morning to bedtime in December, I get my weekly shots wearing the costume. It is fun to see my picture posted with my sleeves pushed up getting my injection. The nurses keep it up all year to show the children who need shots that Santa is brave enough and maybe to remind them that Santa sees what is happening in that office, too.

My favorite cardiologist has a little different view. He is Jewish and he loves Santa. He has made sure the camera is ready every year for twelve or more years. He bounces around and tells the patients he'll be back as soon as he has seen Santa. He has a large office with over 10 people serving as staff, both medical and clerical and they have all enjoyed Santa's visit each year.

Then last year, the doctor came to the lunch room where I was talking to the physician's assistant and where others were waiting for their turn on Santa's lap and announced in a loud voice, "My girls can no longer sit on Santa's lap! Last year they asked for babies and I had to hire more people to cover the maternity leaves. Do not sit on Santa's lap." With a wink and a grin, he left.

Not sure how to tell that last comment to my wife, I just repeated the doctor's words with a smile. She caught the double entendre, but smiled anyway. Santa has been given credit for bringing exotic cars, vacations, husbands and now…babies. I take no credit for the babies. God gets credit for the babies.

The Good Kids List

When my beard was finally white enough to wear without the fake whiskers over it, I realized that all the pictures of me as Santa were out dated. We had just come into the digital age at that time, so I asked my wife to take some pictures of me in front of the Christmas tree in the Santa suit wearing my own hair.

The pictures were promising but lacking something. I got an idea and went to a tall stuffed Santa in my collection and got the long aged parchment list from his hand to hold for my portrait.

That picture, with the list, has become one of our favorites. We use it on the letterhead for North Pole Ministries, our charity. It is on the website. I imagine it is plastered over a thousand beds for sick people and little children.

There are several stories about the list, but the first time I thought of how to use it came to distract a little girl who had come with her mom to have their tax return prepared by my daughter. Those things take a lot of time and must seem boring from the beginning for a little girl. She was obviously well mannered but I could see her mother getting tense as she wiggled. Thinking to distract her, I typed her name in big red letters at the top of the list in the picture.

Then I sent it from my computer to print on the printer just by the little girls shoulder. She jumped a little when the machine began to work seemingly by magic. Then she looked at the picture of Santa emerging from the printer. She was still very conscious of not disturbing her mother who was busy.

I had maneuvered my chair so that I could see her around the office partition. I watched as her eyes got very big when she saw her name coming out of the machine. Finally her excitement was so much that she had to share.

"Mommy", she said politely. "Mommy" more assertively. Finally, "MOMMY, you have to look at my name!"

Her mother was suitably impressed, too, that her child's name was at the top of the Good Kids List in Santa's hand. Their reaction made me think of all the people in this world that serve us without recognition. Many of us have a wall of appreciation or membership certificates. Some of us have "bragging" walls filled with pictures of celebrities shaking our hands. But the vast majority of people have no recognition at all.

So I began finding out the names of the people in stores and offices where I go throughout the year. Then at Christmas, I print dozens and dozens of colored pictures of Santa Claus holding the Good Kids List with their name printed very large, in red letters at the TOP.

When I go to those offices or stores as Santa in December, I have a list with their name at the top to give them. Most of the pictures and lists stay up all year in their cubicles, over the slicing machine in the deli, in the restaurant waiting area or wherever the recipient wants it to be to remember a time of recognition for themselves.

The only ones I put up myself are in hospitals. I post the Good Kids List on the wall where the patient can see it and I make a big deal about telling the nurse to take special care of this patient who is at the head of The Good Kids List.

All the preceding story is true, but the story of the original long list in the stuffed Santa's hand is one to bring a tear to the eye of any parent or grandparent whose dear child has grown up.

When he was about 3 years old, our grandson wanted to make a list of the toys he wanted to send to Santa. My wife dutifully paged through the catalogues with him until he had chosen many essential toys. She showed him the list she had been making as they went along, but he shook his head, "No" he said.

"I wanted my list to be long!"

"No problem" she said and began to hit "return" in between each toy to make a page that had to be taped together before we faxed it to the print shop who gladly received our Santa list each year.

Knowing that the list needed to be long, she sat with our grandson and they made a list of people we should pray for. It started with his great grandparents, grandparents, mom, friends, neighbors, Sunday school teachers and anyone he could remember. The list was very long. (She remembered to hit "return" between each name.)

The list was so long it needed to be in the hands of the biggest Santa in my collection. This stuffed Santa was almost as tall as the little boy who helped tape it together and placed it in his hands. He was happy and so were we.

A year later, a dog's tail swished the list out of Santa's hand and onto the floor. When I stooped to pick it up to put it back, I noticed someone had been writing with a pen on the list. At first, I was dismayed that our precious remembrance had been defaced, but then we realized that the little boy had grown up enough to read the names himself. He had placed a large check mark by each name. He never mentioned it to us in all these years.

He prayed for the people on that list with his mother for years. Now he prays by himself. The list is still there in Santa's hand, 20 years later.

This Visit Surprised A Lot of People

"I was feeling terrible. Lying in that hospital bed when I wanted to be at home was no fun either" the elderly tiny Jewish lady began. "I already knew my family would not be able to visit because their business in another city would keep them working 20 hours a day until Christmas. So, I admit to feeling a little sorry for myself."

"My attitude must have been apparent to the nurses because it seemed they were making a special effort to be cheerful, but respectful of my religion by not shouting 'Ho, Ho, Ho' as I heard them doing in other rooms."

"I was lying there just thinking about my husband who had died recently after a long illness and missing his being beside me in that dreary room. The nurse was about to start a procedure I wouldn't enjoy when we heard bells."

"I wonder what that can be" she asked looking around toward the hall doorway.

"That is a visitor for me" I said calmly.

"I don't think so, ma'am. I think that might be a Santa Claus coming to wish someone a Merry Christmas."

"Yes it is," I said "he is coming to see me"!

"To say she looked surprised and skeptical would both be understatements. Not wanting to argue with a patient, however, she smiled and kept looking at the door as the bells got louder."

"HO, HO, HO" I called out as I reached her doorway. "May I come in"?

Evelyn was lying in a bed that made her look tiny and frail. I enjoyed her smile and I especially enjoyed the look on the face of her nurse. Bewildered, I think.

Once she grasped the fact that I had truly come to see Evelyn, she left the room for us to have some privacy. Evelyn was really enjoying telling me the story I had only guessed.

"After you left, all the nurses and aides came into my room to ask about how a Jewish lady knew Santa and to see my stuffed animals and my name at the top of the 'Good Kids List' you had hung on my wall.

"I had such a good time telling them about being your neighbor for over twenty five years and hearing those same bells every December day for all that time. I could see their skepticism begin to wane after a bit. It was a lot of fun and your visit did cheer me up quite a bit."

"I don't look forward to Christmas, but all that it represents for us, family, love, joy, thoughtfulness, kindness, and peace is part of my religion, too. You brought all that to me again in my hospital bed."

"Oh, thank your family again for saving me so I could be in the hospital at all."

I remembered the day that our young Grandson had gone to her home to clean her patio for her. She had not been feeling well so he took her some cans of chicken soup and ginger ale. We had been neighbors for years before he was born, but could not share or borrow food because they kept a kosher home. Canned items were an exception. She was sick.
He usually was gone about a hour helping her with tasks outside her home, but this day he came back yelling for his mother to "Come Quick. She is on the floor."

Our family went into action then. Our Grandson called 911 and did a good job until they asked about her medications. Our daughter was looking everywhere for bottles, but couldn't find them, even in her purse. She used speed dial and reached her daughter long distance who solved the problem.

We could hear the sirens, but they were circling us! I knew the city had a confusing numbering system that included her house so I went outside and eventually with a big light signaled the ambulance and paramedics to the right house.

Evelyn remained unconscious through the paramedic treatment and the ride to the hospital. The worst part for her would have been the horrible mess those huge firefighters left in her kitchen…blood, wrappers, used bandages, stripped off gloves. Even in illness her home had been spotless. We were glad she never knew.

Our daughter was in the ambulance with her to be certain to know where she was taken and to be able to call back the frantic daughter with any news.

The doctors told us that if she had not been able to open her door for our grandson that little bit before she collapsed and if he had not gotten help for her immediately, she would have died or been permanently damaged. That is what Evelyn was thanking us for… getting her to the hospital.

This is the same neighbor who was so reluctant to sit on Santa's lap about 20 years earlier.

Lost Boys of Sudan

Santa made a special trip to visit each of our special adopted Lost Boys at their jobs that first Christmas after they came to America. They knew me well and called me "Father John" the African term of respect for an elder friend or family member.

They had entry level positions commanding little respect from their fellow workers but I knew how much attention those same workers would pay to the person Santa came to visit. I wanted these young men to have something to make them feel special in their work environment where they had to rely on co-workers to teach them simple culture based actions. Their friends loved the visit, but each one of the Lost Boys simply laughed out loud to see me in such a strange suit. The last thing you learn in a new language and a new culture is the jokes. They wanted to fit in so they laughed.

We each tried to tell them about Santa Claus. You know the story, on Christmas Eve Santa visits every boy and girl in the world bringing them toys and candy….<u>Wait!</u>

These boys didn't have toys. They didn't even have enough food. They had no home after age 5. They were hunted by animals and soldiers and 2 of every 3 who fled the home villages in Sudan had died by the time they reached the UN refugee camp in Kenya called Kakama.

During the 1000 mile walk they swam rivers with crocodiles, passed through 4 countries that could not continue supporting them, fled new wars, ate mud & grass and barely survived.

Small acts of kindness increased their trust in their new American lives. The excitement they saw around their job sites after their personal visit from Santa helped these young men realize that life is not all harsh reality.

There would be years of struggle ahead for them learning this new culture, job expectations, retirement plans, apartments, citizenship, and university, marriage and parenthood. But survival at the basic level was behind them when they were chosen by the US State Department to legally come to the US.

My dream and the dream of my family as we helped many, especially 11, acclimate to society in Phoenix, AZ is that they will remain grounded but learn to understand and enjoy the dreams and joy of the childhood they never had.

Santa Without the Suit

100 Lost Boys of the Sudan found their way to All Saints Episcopal Church that summer of 2001. Along their 1000 mile walk seeking survival in Africa they stayed a while in Somalia where a wonderful Episcopal missionary made sure they were all baptized and had chosen a Christian name…from the Bible which was in English. So we met a lot of boys named Jacob, John, & James.

In Kakama refugee camp where they lived for 10 years, they continued having Episcopal services so it was natural that they looked for a church where they would be accepted. All Saints Church volunteers helped them at all levels acclimate to this society. We helped them complete their shots when their social service agency did not finish their responsibility to them, we helped equip their apartments, we found jobs and helped them enroll in schools.

God gave my family a heart for Africa and these Sudanese fit right into it. My family adopted 3 apartments of boys, a total of 11. Catholic Social Services chose the housing, gave each a mattress on the floor, 1 cup, 1 chair, 1 plate and food for 1 week. They were to get food stamps as a loan until their paychecks came. They were still very hungry. Many did not have enough food at first and some were afraid of getting lost without help. We gave them all of that.

They flocked to us on September 11, 2001 because they were all confused and because some of them were working checkpoints at the airport when the planes were grounded. They had questions spawned by TV coverage like "What is Secret Service?"

They felt better being together and enjoyed being able to teach us something they had learned in their long walk to freedom. "We do not understand your countrymen. We are telling you not to trust the Arabs. Yet you are surprised at this treachery against you. We are not understanding you or other Americans."

After church services on the patio "our" Lost Boys brought their friends from other apartments to us when they had problems. Consequently many of them had our business cards so they could call us when they needed help.

One night after dinner a much stressed Lost Boy called asking for Father John. We could barely understand him because half the words were in Dinka, their tribal language. We understood finally that there had been an accident and the cab they had hired to take them to their job had had no seat belts. Several were thrown out of the vehicle and 2 were taken by helicopter to a "presidential hospital". The others were going to a closer hospital. Would Father John please help the ones in the air?

We guessed they may have been taken to John C Lincoln hospital, the only presidential connection we knew. After calling the location nearest the accident, my daughter, Stefanie, could hear yelling in Dinka in the phone. She began asking questions but the nurse kept demanding that we tell her the name of the patient. We didn't know the names; we didn't know the boys; we were just offering to help if we could.

Once the nurse realized that we "knew" about them, she begged us to come to help. When I went into the ER I found one flailing and yelling with a bad head injury. I had not been worried I would recognize the injured Lost Boys. All of them are from the Dinka tribe in South Sudan. They are very tall, very thin, and so black their skin takes up the light when you take their pictures.

I smiled at him and he smiled back recognizing me somehow. I assured him that I would stay or have someone guard his organs. "In America," I stretched the truth, "we have no need for your organs. No one here will take your organs while you sleep."

I asked the nurse for another sheet for him. As soon as he got it, he wrapped it around his head and went immediately quiet. That is the way they went to sleep as little boys on their long walk. The sheet or shirt or cloth kept the deadly bugs from their ears and faces while they slept on the ground. In a way, it was like a security blanket.

Stefanie spoke with the other Dinka Lost Boy who was not so seriously injured, but very worried about his friend. She got their names to make the hospital happy and then explained to the staff their fear of being in the hospital without their family to protect them from having their organs stolen. These African young men had never been in a hospital before and had heard horrible stories of neglect and abuse, but they trusted us that we would not let them be "hurt" by the doctors.

We made several calls and got more church volunteers to go to the other hospital where Lost Boys were being treated and we found some of their friends to come to stay with these at Lincoln hospital.

Santa did not wear his suit that night in October, but the nurses and doctors all commented that I looked like Santa. They said they had noticed the resemblance when I was bent over to help & reassure everyone like Santa would. I always have my Santa business cards with me and some of them were not surprised at all when they looked and saw my face and the Santa Suit on the business card that reads, "North Pole Ministries".

North Pole Ministries

For over 25 years this Santa Claus operated as an outreach ministry of All Saints Episcopal Church. The donations people made in thanksgiving for what Santa had done for them and to support what they knew of Santa's mission were sufficient each year to pay for the expenses for candy canes and stuffed toys.

Occasionally Santa needed a new suit so he never looked shabby or worn. My costume cost over $800 when it was complete and that was more money in the 1970's than it is now. In addition to the red velvet and beautiful fur, patent leather and dance bells, I wore out 8 sets of white haired beards and wigs until God and nature gave me the perfect color growing out of my own head.

When Fr. Carlozzi retired as rector of our church to become the Chaplin of the Phoenix Fire Department, it left the church with several years of temporary, interim leadership. There is a long search process in the Episcopal church for new rectors and it usually takes several years to accomplish. During that time, the financial office did not want to continue the necessary accounting for the Santa donations and placed the money into the general funds.

For all those years people knew their donations were tax deductible and we felt forced to make sure their beliefs remained true to insure the continuation of the Santa ministry.

With prayer, my family and I organized a Board of Directors, wrote Articles of Incorporation for a Non-profit Organization and applied to Internal Revenue Service for federal non-profit status as a 501 (c)(3) organization called North Pole Ministries. Our application was approved by IRS in under 30 days, a record time tax professionals say!

Our ministry was enlarged beyond just Santa Claus at this time. We became a Working Poor Charity under Arizona Department of Revenue law. Our working poor of choice have been refugees from many nations and creeds. We hope they are all legal immigrants, but Santa cannot ask a child on his knee "Does your Mommy have a green card?"

We have paid rent for injured or ill, bought prescriptions in emergencies, and provided food for many families on a temporary basis. This year we've been called on to give a little interim help to two families whose homes have burned. The first family escaped from their fire with only pajamas. Everyone needed clothes to go to church with their pastor Mother on Easter Sunday. We've bought beds, linens, Microwave ovens and other items people need in a hurry.

People and businesses have donated old computers and components to us over the past 10 years. Our grandson, Johnathan, refurbishes them until they meet the requirements for a college applicant, We load basic software and donate the computer, monitor and printer unit to refugees and others who want to apply to college.

We did not count the units we have refurbished, but we believe we have given over 100 complete sets to individuals and groups.

Our updated computers have been used to set up computer labs at several housing complexes for working poor families so that the children can use them in the after school homework programs they run.

Johnathan is the little boy who ushered me to my own front door many years ago. He has grown up with Santa Claus and began helping in many ways as he was capable. There is another story about Johnathan, our second Santa Claus.

The best story during the transition to North Pole Ministries happened after a "rejection" letter from the State of Arizona. We had received non=profit, tax exempt status from the Internal Revenue Service. The State of Arizona where we live, has a credit for specific contributions individuals make to some non-profit charities like ours that benefit the working poor of our state. The State had appointed someone from the Department of Revenue to review financial records of all the thousands of charities claiming to serve the working poor. The rule is that at least HALF of all charity expenses must go to directly help people who qualify under the definition of working poor with items necessary for their daily living..

We knew we met that criteria so our daughter, Stefanie, an Enrolled Agent and known by many at our taxing authority, called to inquire about our rejection. "Toys and candy are not essentials for life!" our compliance officer said. "I have been to your website and I see what you do with Santa Claus. Those activities are fun and nice, but they are NOT essential to life." If she had been with me sometimes, she would not have made that statement, however, Stefanie responded by asking her to go to the other pages of the website.

There she found the information about providing food, clothing, RX, medical, beds and things really essential to life. She was won over and reversed her previous determination leaving us again a qualifying working poor charity.

The truly funny part of this story is coming, however. She told Stefanie that she was giving away her entire collection of Beanie Babies and asked if we would like to have them. Accepting gracefully, Stefanie asked if she would like us to pick them up.

"Oh, no," she said "I'll send them to you at the next big meeting of the Arizona Forum for Improvement of Taxation."

The following week, Stefanie and her mother heard a very loud voice from behind them as they sat waiting for the conference to begin, "Stefanie. Ellen. I hope you are here. I have something big for you. Stefanie. Ellen."

When they turned, silhouetted in the open doorway to the conference room was the Assistant Director of the entire Department of Revenue holding out on either side of him two huge trash bags. He looked like Santa himself, but not as jolly.

You guessed it. He was delivering the Beanie Babies. 150 tax professionals watched him deliver the stuffed toys as they waited to hear him speak from the podium in the seminar program with his voice of authority from the State of Arizona.

From rejection to donation. North Pole Ministries continues with God's blessing (and another from the State of Arizona).

HAROLD

North Pole Ministries is an IRS approved 501(c)(3) charity. As a corporation our board of directors meets and plans and approves items of income and expenses that further our tax exempt goals.

Until I met Harold. I had known his grandmother for years because she was in charge of the party for one of my favorite organizations. The people who attend the party bring their families and enjoy being together and introducing their families to their friends in their disease support group.

Each year I asked about her family and usually she said, "Fine" like we often do. But last year, she got a little teary and said, "My little grandson has been so sick and he is in the hospital again. His mother is on disability and we just know we cannot afford the only toy he wants this year. It is really expensive, but nothing else will do. I'm sorry for bothering you, but it is hard to think of anything else right now."

He was four years old and had been hospitalized 5 times that fall. His birth defect involved his digestive system, but he was still being tested. Without consulting anyone on the board I heard myself saying, "Don't worry about the toy. Santa will get a Crusher for you to give Harold on Christmas morning. We'll work out a time later. What hospital is he in?"

The cutest little boy was sitting in his bed when I walked into the hospital room. He knew it must be Santa because he heard the bells so he sat up and waited for me. I gave him a candy cane and stuffed animal and told him I knew it was hard to be good when he was hurting. "I'll be back to see you on Christmas Eve," I told him as I left with a hearty "Ho, Ho, Ho" for his nurses.

His mother followed me out to my car and retrieved the Crusher to place in her own trunk for Christmas…at home or hospital. Harold would be happy.

I felt so good about giving that child the delight of his heart. It is difficult to explain how he began to exemplify for me all the personal special little boys in my own life. I was happy for him and prayed for his return to good health.

Months later, I learned that his diagnosis was made by a hospital in another state. They found that his colon was too long! Six times longer than it should be! His entire day was spent eating and exercising and trying to figure out a regime that would keep him out of the hospital. It didn't always work.

When you don't feel good, when you hurt, it is hard to jump around and run. Still it is necessary for his health.

This year he needed a Wii Fitness…the interactive gaming system with golf, car racing, field and track, tennis, bowling etc. Each scenario requires your own physical activity to play the game. With such a video game at home, Harold was much more likely to get up and move even when he was hurting too much to run and play like a normal 6 year old..

The doctors had explained that his own physical activity was the best medicine to keep his body functioning correctly. Our hope was that Harold would be excited to play enough to get him on his feet and help him stay out of the hospital.

Santa knows a lot about shopping, but this time he needed help to buy the Wii and make sure all the components worked together. Johnathan helped me select the compatible components and a few extra fitness games, but the whole family had fun testing each part before we delivered the system. I was certainly glad we had found all the "bugs" in the systems we had selected before I took the gift to Harold's mother.

She reported that Harold loved his exercise program now. He worked out before school, kept active after school and didn't mind jumping around even when his stomach hurt.

God created Harold and when his body wasn't perfect, he gave a great idea to someone who created Wii.

Santa's Regular Visits in December

I will visit anyone who is sick or dying, especially a child. I have even put on the heavy suit and all the fake hair and beard in July without regard to the 118 degree temperatures to visit a hospital when someone needs my special brand of cheer.

In December, I have a filled calendar of events before Thanksgiving. I visit Youth Centers and Boys and Girls Clubs, Firemen and their special projects, Churches, schools, drug prevention programs for kids and more. There are parties for support groups, office staff, doctors, migrant families, even country clubs.

People think my four wheeled vehicle is a magic sleigh when they try to schedule their event without regard to rush hour traffic or great distances. Often when my schedule calls me to be across town or way north, I stop in to see customers, friends or merchants located nearby.

We got a call yesterday from a law firm nearby asking if Santa was coming this year because they wanted to plan their Christmas party around my visit. If I forget someone one year, they are disappointed and let me know they felt forgotten.

I wear the costume to McDonald's and put a candy cane in the hand of the cashier. They show everyone else working in the restaurant. Soon the window is filled with hands asking for candy. Then I give the one who helped me a little stuffed animal. The others don't usually ask for more of those, but sometimes they ask for someone who is sick. "Please Santa; I will give it to them."

Sometimes I get the right order in my bag.

The people in our favorite Chinese restaurant are Buddhist, but if I forget to go in as Santa, they are terribly disappointed. I go to each booth and table, asking if their customers are enjoying their dinner and giving them a candy cane for later.

The "good ole boys" at the barbeque restaurant love Santa, too. They want to give me a beer and a rack of ribs. Can you imagine what this white fur and beard would look like after a pile of ribs? And nobody wants to see a drunken Santa so I never drink anything but water while wearing the costume.

When I went into the tiny gourmet bakery we have come to love, the baker gave me a gorgeous caramel brownie in a box. I was happy because I could take it home safely to enjoy later while not wearing red velvet and white fur. Our baker was surprised that I had come to see her at Christmas just to bring her a little bear.

I didn't go in for the brownie, but it often happens that I leave with a little gift. I think giving me something makes merchants feel better about accepting the personalized cheer they find from my Santa visit. I try to be gracious with all gifts they offer. (Except as noted above.) This one was easy and delicious.

I always stop at the dry cleaner. He needs to be my friend for emergencies like I mentioned in another story. His customers and workers are happy to see Santa and love hearing that my suit looks as good as it does thanks to them. I remind them that I will be coming back soon with 4 Santa suits and bags that will need cleaning.

We don't expect gifts or free things when I go to make the Santa visits. I go for an entirely different reason. I go to express my gratitude for good service, for friendship, for compassion, and competent service throughout the years.

Some people have been customers, some still are, but I try not to forget the "old" ones either when I am driving to my scheduled visits all over this wide valley.

I fit in the serendipitous stops at merchants when I have a little extra time in their area of town. As I drive past their business, I remember that the owner has been sick or that someone inside was getting a divorce.
 They tell me their problems throughout the year, as though I was still wearing the Santa suit, when I am in their store buying their products or services.

As our clients get older sometimes they start to mail their tax information to us instead of coming in for their appointment. I remembered one afternoon that one of those people was quite ill and I was in his neighborhood. I stopped by and found that they were not at home, but I left a stuffed bear for them with a grandchild. The note I got from them really touched my heart as the bear had touched theirs.

The note explained that their baby great grandchild had heart surgery the day before I left the little bear with them and they felt such peace that he would recover when they saw my bear. The bear was holding between his two paws a big red heart that read, "I love you". God is with me as I travel. He helps me make the decisions about stopping. You could say that he is the great scheduler.

Sometimes the regular visits get me in trouble. Because of the weekend when Christmas fell one year, I had fewer days in December that businesses were working. I stopped at the paper company just minutes after they had closed and missed them entirely that year. In January, when our business buys a lot of paper to do our mailing, I was really in trouble.

No sooner had I opened the door to the store than the assistant manager put her hands on her hips and said "You forgot us this year, Santa. We are all disappointed. I don't know if we have time to give you the special help selecting all your paper colors like we do each year."

She turned away, but not before I had caught the little grin on her face and on the faces of the others behind the counter. I went back outside to my car where I had left a few stuffed animals. I had thought this would happen. Without the suit, I went in bearing animals and candy canes and said, "Ho, Ho, HO. Merry Christmas and Happy New Year."

I was forgiven.

Every Dentist Needs a Santa By The Chair.

The coliseum building in Phoenix is old and more likely to be used for a rodeo than for basketball and hockey, I could hardly believe my eyes when I first saw it converted into a tremendous dental clinic with hundreds of dental chairs. For two days in December it is sanitized, electrified and equipped with the latest dental equipment. It is staffed with volunteer dentists, surgeons, hygienists, assistants and all other supporting staff necessary to provide one stop dental service to hundreds of people who cannot afford dental care. All dental services for those 2 days are performed for FREE.

I was amazed again today when I went for my fourth visit to this massive dental clinic. It may take a while, but each person is evaluated and moves through a sequence of care stations to receive what he needs. They do x-rays, surgery, extractions, make bridges, fill teeth and make dentures while the people wait!

At least 500 people have spent the night outside in the cold to insure their place in line for the free dental service. Many of them are in pain. In spite of the gratitude of these people who could not afford dentistry any other way, many of them are apprehensive. I admit that I feel apprehensive on the day of my dental appointments and can even be said to be a little anxious about having some pain.

These poor people may not have seen a dentist in a long while and they are dreading what the news will be. They don't think it will be good news and they worry. Kids cry because they sense the anxiety of other patients.

Today was fun because when I arrived there was a large group of at least 40 in one section waiting their turn for the next stage in the process. Seated beside them was another group of 40 or 50 waiting for something else.

I walked up and said, "Ho, HO, HO. This group is the good kids. This group is..."

Before I could even start another word, the second group was shouting...all together, "No! Santa we are the good kids! They are the bad kids".

The first group assured me that they were really good. The interesting part of the response is that all these people were strangers that morning. Yet they showed remarkable camaraderie and unity when vying for Santa's good graces.

The important thing is that for a few minutes, they forgot to be anxious or worried about what the dentist would find to do in their mouth. Distraction. Fun. Smiles. Hugs. That is what Santa spends two days doing for the dental patients.

God has worked a miracle in this Santa's heart that has translated into my being able to help in some amazing ways these days. I mentioned earlier that I admit to some apprehension before my dental appointments. I didn't admit that I had skipped a few years of dental care myself because of an intense gag reflex and severe apprehension. My new dentist promised they had gas and sedation dentistry if I needed it and I have caught up on needed dental care.

I have also not admitted that I do not like the sight of blood or injections. I used to cringe. I used to get queasy and faint. I used to gag. I used to leave.

Now God's miracle in me lets me joke with men and console women and kids while their procedures are beginning or ongoing.

The doctors and nurses send runners through the huge building to find me when they have a "problem" patient of any age. Sometimes the patients are so frightened that they can't open their mouth all the way. Sometimes they are sobbing or screaming. They want treatment, but they are really afraid.

Part of the miracle that God has given to me is that I can encourage, distract, love, comfort the patient enough that the doctors and assistants can reach in and get their job done. Once the anesthetic is begun, it doesn't hurt any more and I can tell a joke, hand them a stuffed animal and wave goodbye.

When I told my wife about the event this year, she could scarcely believe her ears! I was describing a woman who needed a lot of care and how the dentist had gotten a chair for me to sit by her as he worked. I promised her I would hold her hand while he extracted her tooth. I described the cracking sound, the bleeding, the actual extraction and what I was saying to her while the dentist worked. My wife asked me if she had to clean the Santa suit because I had gotten sick.

"No", I said. "God has healed me of my queasy stomach when I am helping calm the dental patients".

I give away about 1800 stuffed animals over the course of the two days. Everyone I see gets a candy cane and the dentists don't seem to mind.

There were more than 1500 dental volunteers, 2000 patients and then there was Santa. God oversaw it all.

When Santa Cannot Hug

Every story I have told includes hugs, by the dozens. I love giving the hugs and receiving the ones from the little children who are so happy to see me. I feel like the hugs convey the love of Jesus to the ones I hug.

The hardest visits I make, then, are the ones when I cannot hug the children. Last week was a recent example of how I leave the visit having brought a little cheer, but with tears in my heart.

I was at the Phoenix Children's Hospital, invited by a specific group who were giving a party for some of the children their volunteers help. Their children are usually confined for a long time and have semi-permanent ports in their bodies.

The port area must be kept very clean, of course, but it is ugly and makes the children self-conscious. This group provides hospital gowns made specifically to insure that the ports are covered for cleanliness and an attempt at fashion.

I arrived and greeted the volunteers. I met worried parents and we took a lot of pictures. We waited until the medical staff came to check us into the unit. I was given specific instructions! <u>Do Not Touch The Children</u>! No Hugs! <u>NO HUGS</u>!
  Most of the children have cancer. The instructions were for THEIR health...not mine. I might be carrying germs that could harm them. With a sad heart, I promised, "No Hugs".

Once I was in the unit I realized I would not be allowed into any of the children's rooms. I was to be the "Santa in the hall". I was determined to pray for each child, even silently.

One child was only 3 months old and was born with leukemia. Staff got pictures for his family. Many of the children had no hair due to their chemotherapy. We got pictures the best that we could. Some were out of bed and playing a little and acted excited to see me. We took pictures with me standing at the door and the camera looking past me to see the smiling child. I was allowed to hand out stuffed animals to some of the children. Some of the families let me pray for their child's restoration with them.

A lot of children had family with them in their room waiting with a camera. I would kneel down in the doorway, the child would come close to me and turn around looking into the room for their family to take a perfect picture with Santa.

I stayed several hours and reached every child that I could with a candy cane. Much of the ministry that day was to the parents and the harried staff. I pray that the children who saw me that day will remember those moments of happiness even when they are lonely and feeling bad.

Many years ago when I was in this hospital, nurses would come to get me and take me all around to see particular children or visit patient units.

 From there I could visit where I had been invited. Today new laws prevent the staff from inviting me for an unscheduled visit with anyone. But the law does not prevent me from praying as I walk to each room.

The only children I saw that day were in the cancer unit and in the lobby.

I was glad to have had the long wait in the lobby before the medical staff came to get the volunteers because it was a busy place that day. Parents brought children to see doctors and receive treatment. Whole families came to visit their sick child. We took pictures of children in wheelchairs, with IV poles and candy canes. Families came to get pictures with children and parents and Santa.

Seeing Santa brought a little joy and cheer to families and staff that day. My visit lightened the mood for a while. God gave hope to the people that another Christmas would be brighter.

Through the tears in my heart, I prayed for the children as I walked through the hospital. I prayed for God's healing.

JOHNATHAN, our Second Santa

You have met my grandson, Johnathan, in other stories beginning with his first visit from Santa where he showed me the door to leave. He is also the one who identified the scrawny wooly moose as the desired CHET.

There is another piece to the story of Johnathan's first official visit from Santa. He was just about to turn three years old. You remember that I had given him gifts and candy from my bag. He was happy and running around showing his gifts to his mother and grandmother. Then he disappeared. I was so tired that I just sat on the sofa, glad that I was finished for the evening.

Then Johnathan came running back into the living room carrying a small drawstring bag he had had in his room. He was so excited! He had filled his bag with small toys from his room and proceeded to run to each one of us giving us each two toys from his little bag until it was emptied. Then he grinned and took my hand and showed me to the front door.

That was one of the first demonstrations of Johnathan's generous heart we had seen so dramatically demonstrated. In the midst of his special night, his first visit from Santa Claus, he gave of his only treasure to insure that we all had something "wonderful", too.

Over the years of his life he has assumed a lot of roles helping Santa as he was capable at different ages. He was about seven when he went with me to the party for the developmentally handicapped adults at the church. To be certain that he was safe, I put him immediately behind me so he couldn't get out to wander into the night. He wore a Santa Hat and a red shirt. His job was to hand me a package of a candy cane and a stuffed animal as each person was getting up from my lap. He did a good job for a long time. Then I was digging into the bags for myself to find the gifts.

My wife was in the back of the impossibly crowded room and she could see us, but not get to us through the people. She took a picture, however. There is Johnathan, giving himself a break. He had hung his hat on a doorknob and was leaning back, licking a candy cane secure in his corner.

Over the years he has spent days and days at big events handing me many thousands of animals and candy to help speed the lines of children waiting to talk to Santa. Some events had over 600 children and I always felt grateful when Johnathan could go along to help me. He got no glory, no recognition. People only have eyes for Santa, even the staff of the event. No one thanked him for all that he did lifting boxes and digging in the bags for animals. No one but me. I've always been grateful. On a few occasions where the food was great, he felt rewarded. I explained that we were serving these people as Jesus commanded. We were doing it to help people know God's love.

"Lord, when did we see You hungry and feed you or thirsty and give You drink?...And the King will answer and say to them, 'Assuredly, I say to you, inasmuch as you did it to one of the least of these My brethren, you did it to me'" Matthew 25: 38-40

When he was young, Johnathan helped me select the specific animals we bought to give. We needed 3,000 to 7,000 each year. It was good to have his input because he knew what kids his age wanted.

As he grew into a strong young man, he has taken a lot of the responsibility for lifting the boxes of animals that fill our two car garage. He lifts them as we sort them for each group; he lifts them as we load them into the van before an event; often he lifts them with me at the event venue to place them near the Santa chair; he lifts them into the attic for storage when they are left Christmas night. God has blessed me with a healthy back for most of these years and he certainly blesses me with Johnathan's good back.

Before the large events Johnathan drives one of our vans loaded with animals to the venue and we unload the two vans into the party room. We place signs on the boxes that read "Santa knows who is naughty and nice." The picture of Santa, the goodness of people and the blessing of God have kept our boxes of animals secure for the intended children all these years.

Since I have a red cell phone some children have asked about Bernard, the head elf in the Santa Claus movies. One day I got the idea to call home to see if Bernard was available to talk to this "kid", a developmentally handicapped man of about 60. Johnathan answered and without skipping a beat, became Bernard. Every time I call, unless he is taking an exam, he is generous enough to spend time with the child waiting eagerly to explain the specifics of the toy he needs for Christmas.

The developmentally handicapped individuals believe the movies and stories they see are real life. When they are talking to
Bernard, they are certain they are placing their order directly to the North Pole. Onlookers stare in awe at their response to Bernard. The mystique of the season and the party atmosphere create memories for a lifetime.

Johnathan grew to be over six feet tall in high school. He has his own velvet and fur Santa suit. But the school required that he be clean shaven. He wears the fake, but beautiful, white beard and wig and hates how hot it makes him. In spite of that he makes a great Santa! I described in an earlier story how Santa should look. Johnathan looks grand! He is tall and straight. Since the American public prefers a slender Santa today, he fits the bill perfectly.

We really needed his services several times over his adult years. I have had 3 major surgeries and cancer. Each time he filled in at places desperate for a Santa.

People thought he was an adult. He did such a good job that they would call for him to make more appearances, but sometimes his mother would decline stating that he had to take his high school exams. People were really shocked to learn that he was so young.

For three years of high school Johnathan attended the party for the school faculty as Santa. He gave each teacher a stuffed animal and a candy cane. They didn't give him a chance to tell stories, exactly, but they were very curious about who he was. Usually they were quite surprised if they learned he was a student...especially if he was one of their own!

The best animal we ever bought, we bought for the teachers at St. Mary's High School. It was a deep green velvet bear. He had always given something with the school colors, but that green bear remains everyone's favorite.

One year the football team asked Johnathan to be their Santa when they went to a school for migrant workers' kids. The football team had adopted several grades for Christmas gifts and a party and Johnathan went on the school bus with them to distribute the gifts. As usual with Santa, he got no food, but he got the great enjoyment of having the kids there love him and follow him each step he took.

The only public recognition Johnathan has ever received for all his years of working for Santa and North Pole Ministries was at his senior honors program.

He received the award for the Most Christian Service Hours in the entire Senior Class for their whole 4 years. We are all very proud of his hours working for us and the other charities that he served.

Johnathan fields phone calls about donations for North Pole Ministries and scheduling events with Santa. He built the current website and maintains it. He finds my Santa letters when I lose them in my computer and keeps the computer working when I "break" it.

Johnathan is still young to be on the board of North Pole Ministries, but we consult him and listen to his advice and suggestions for ministry. I don't see how we could continue running North Pole Ministries without his help.

We thank God for Johnathan. He has a big heart and loving compassion for people. I know he prays for us. We pray for him as he lives God's will for his life.

"Let us never tire of doing good." Galatians 6:9
"When it comes to being kind, there is no limit. The nature of love is to give and to do good continually. Love never tires or gives up, even faced with setbacks and difficulties. You, too, will learn to love and to do good without ceasing, if the love of Jesus is really in your heart and shines out of you." M Basilea Schlink. <u>More Precious than Gold.</u>

Fireman's Santa

More than thirty years ago was the first time I was invited to the Glendale Youth Center for their Christmas party. Their building was small. Their program had not been running long, but they had a lot of enthusiasm to help the kids in their barrio neighborhood.

The program was at night to include a small supper. It was one of the coldest nights I've ever experienced in Phoenix in 35 years and my chair was by the door! I can get really hot in the Santa suit, but that night it was not warm enough!

My family was there to help if needed and they reported that kids and parents were lined up around the building and down the block. It was so early in the Santa ministry that we did not have stuffed animals or gifts to give, only candy canes. That didn't matter to the children! They were so excited! I was excited as I struggled to remember a few words of Spanish to speak to the little ones. That was the first night I learned that language is not essential for communication. Love transcends any language and there was a lot of love that night.

There are beautiful stories about the directors, staff and kids at Christmas parties for the thirty years that I was their Santa on the second Saturday of December. But this story will be about firemen.

The Youth Center party evolved to be a lunch oriented carnival beginning in late morning. Santa rode around the neighborhood on top of a big yellow fire truck with police cars ahead and behind all with sirens and lights flashing to call the people to the Youth Center.

When the city budget was good, the event was huge with over 1,500 children sometimes. Toys for Tots donated gifts. We brought stuffed animals and candy canes. There was free lunch. Usually there were craft booths with face painting and lots of glitter.

Sometimes there was a stage with LOUD music and neighborhood dance groups performing. Always there were police "booths" for touring: SWAT vehicles to climb, canine officer demonstrations, robotic phones and other exciting things for the children to see and lots of literature. "Don't Do Drugs." "Stay In School."

During the year the Glendale Youth Center operated a lot like a Boys and Girls Club with after school programs oriented to teaching and keeping kids busy and out of trouble. Everyone looked forward to December and the big party.

Santa was outside some years in the lovely Arizona sunshine, but some years when the budget was tighter and the free items were only offered to Youth Center members, we were inside.

  It was always well organized and well controlled. I was only mobbed for a short time when I got off the fire truck and then it was bedlam for a few minutes with excited kids of all ages. You can see pictures of these events on our website at northpoleministries.org

My Youth Center Saturday would begin by loading my van full of stuffed animals in case the ones I had delivered the week before were not enough. My family and I drove our two vans to a school parking lot where we would meet the fire truck and police cars. The firemen and women were always excited to be driving Santa. Even the policemen came to get animals and candy canes and pictures with Santa. Then it was time to climb onto the truck.

That was never easy. You see the Santa costume pants are not cut like jeans. They are red velvet costume pants and expensive. With great concentration I could climb the ladder and then I had to wait for the fireman assigned to me to climb up and give me instructions about which hoses to use as my "throne". I carried a large tablecloth to spread out on the hoses to keep my velvet pants protected and I think the firemen were insulted.

The restrictions on having a "passenger" on top of the truck included the provision that a trained fireman be with me at all times. Over the years I had talked to each of them as we drove up and down streets waving and calling to the kids to come to the Youth Center.

One time we spotted a burning palm tree in an alley as we drove the neighborhood. A fire truck does not ignore a fire! "It doesn't matter who is on top, we stop for fires", my young fireman escort said. We stopped and my firemen and women got out to put out the fire. Fortunately it was a small fire and help came so we could proceed to the party. I had a lot of fun telling my worried family that I was OK as I climbed down from the fire truck. "We've been to a FIRE!"

I have always found the firemen and policemen and women to be professional even when they are excited to be helping Santa. They do not forget their duties even as they are smiling and friendly with the children who surround us.

I was not to know that this Saturday was to be one of my last to ever ride the fire truck. The Youth Center would close forever in two years because of a failing city budget.

Nothing was different about the procedure that morning. The fire crew was excited to be "off duty" assigned to drive Santa. We took a lot of pictures at the truck as always. I was very glad to have the young firemen behind me on the ladder as I got older...remember the costume pants challenge.

We got settled on top of the hoses and the ride began. We waved and smiled and chatted and then the young fireman said, "It is really nice that you do this. I came to the Youth Center as a kid and this party meant so much to me!

The lunch and the gifts were a real treat to a boy like me who was raised without any luxuries. My stuffed animal I got from Santa was usually the only gift I got for Christmas".

Wow! He looked young. I knew he wasn't yet thirty. So I asked him, "How old are you, if you don't mind telling me?"

"I'm 23" he said.

"I have been coming to Glendale Youth Center for 30 years," I told him. "I am your Santa".

There might have been tears in his eyes. I couldn't really tell because there were definitely tears in mine.

As soon as the truck stopped, he told his crew the story and they all went to the front of the line of kids waiting to sit on Santa's lap. They had cell phones and my family had a camera and he got another picture of himself sitting on Santa's lap.

God protects the hearts of those who serve and protect us.

How Did I Know This Doctor?

In earlier stories I have told about going to see our health care providers in December to let them know their patients appreciate what they do for us throughout the year. Like anyone else, they can feel overlooked and underappreciated in spite of the details they study to serve each of their patients.

One Christmas season I was in a parking garage of a medical building working in the back of the van arranging animals and stuffing my bag for the next visit. A young doctor in scrubs and surgeon's hat called out, "Hi, Santa".

I turned and smiled and gave him a little stuffed dog with a candy cane. He was stunned. Then he told me he would give it to a nurse at the hospital. "I just left her and she is having a really hard time. I'll take it back to her right now."

When I heard that, I took back my little animal and gave him a much bigger, pinker animal with a twinkle in my eye and said, "OK, but give her this one instead. Tell her Santa says he hopes she feels better soon."

I went on to my next stop, not thinking much of the encounter, until the following December when the same doctor met me in the same garage getting ready to go into the medical building. We smiled, I gave him an animal and a candy cane and he told me his nurse was feeling better.

Two years later I was sitting on an examining table in a new doctor's office dreading what was coming. The new doctor came in and shook my hand, stopped dead in his tracks, and said "I already know you, don't I?"

I was looking at him in the same way wondering where I had seen him before. He looked so familiar, but I had never been in an office like this one.

Then he said, "You are Santa! We met in the parking garage...twice."

Of course I remembered and asked about his nurse. He told me she was fine, but no longer his girlfriend. My wife is used to conversations like this, but she was nervous about the reason for our visit.

The doctor's face became very professional as he told me what was going to happen to me next, how the diagnostic process would proceed and when we would finally know what had to be done. With that, he told his nurses that I was Santa and to treat me really well, and he left.

I don't think I felt better because he knew me as Santa, but I knew that he was the best doctor for my problem. God had arranged that 6 people called me even from Hawaii to talk at length about how he had saved their lives and that he was the best in his field.

I felt confident in his abilities even on the next visit when he walked into the examining room, looked me in the eye and said, "Hi, Santa. You have cancer."

God performed another miracle because after a year of treatment, this Santa was pronounced cancer free. I didn't even miss a Christmas season. I had a lot of background help, but the "Ho, HO, HO's" kept right on.

Pictures with Santa

Since I donned the Santa suit 37 years ago, I have had millions of pictures taken of me. At first people rushed to buy paper cameras, fished cameras out of office cabinets, found dusty Polaroid cameras and used them until the film was gone. In those days we had to squeeze as many people into a small space around me as we could because there was not a lot of film for an unexpected guest.

Over the years I have been filmed for TV many times so I am used to the "live" lights and cameramen or women on the floor trying to get a perfect angle to make a producer happy with the Santa story. I have been photographed a large number of times for newspaper articles. One time it was a beautiful portrait for the cover of the paper's weekly magazine. Other times it was with a cameraman accompanying a reporter who was doing a story about Santa and what he does in December. My story is unusual because I don't sit in a mall where it is easy to find me.

Today people have tiny digital cameras with them in their desks or purses and of course, everyone has a cell phone with a camera. Actually it takes longer now to photograph a group of people because everyone wants someone to take a picture of the group using their own phone. A group of ten means ten pictures on ten cell phones. We all wait cheerfully because we know how important having that picture of Santa can be.

I have found my pictures framed & in nursing homes beside patient bedsides. "How do you know that is you?" staff may ask me if I comment on the picture.

"I can recognize my eyes", I have said for 37 years. Years ago the artificial beard and wig hid most of my face, but my eyes were always there, always blue, and always smiling. I made sure that my lips were smiling under the whiskers so that my eyes would be smiling on top.

People snap pictures surreptitiously as though I will be offended. When I smile at them and offer a candy cane, they usually ask if they can take one with me "to show my child...friend...mother...boyfriend". "They will never believe that I saw Santa!", they say.

I try hard not to turn down any request for pictures, even in the grocery store. Actually, I try to make only one trip to my grocery in December to give little animals to the clerks that help me all year, especially in the bakery and pharmacy. That trip usually takes several hours because of all the pictures that are taken by the staff, managers, and customers. Sometimes I have to shop while in the Santa suit in December and I try to be patient and stop to talk to each little child and wait for pictures.

They post those pictures on facebook and twitter. My pictures are on company websites and personal websites.

You can see me on the covers or pages of charities, associations and businesses publications commemorating their Christmas celebrations or parties. In this day of the "selfie" my picture is on thousands of phones. People keep those pictures a long time, too!

One day I had taken my daughter for outpatient surgery. The nurse was looking at me more than at her. I was wearing a yellow Hawaiian shirt and shorts. My daughter said she was annoyed with the nurse because as a patient she needed attention for her apprehension about surgery, She could tell what was coming because she has grown up with people's reactions to me. "I have your picture on my phone!" the nurse finally said, excitedly. "You are the Santa I saw last year. I still have your picture here!" She produced our picture with me as Santa and proudly showed it to our daughter, the doctors and anyone who would look. Stefanie's surgery went well, anyway.

People don't seem to care how they are dressed or how they look when they see me. They want a picture with Santa. I've seen women with wet hair and lounge robes in the grocery want their picture with Santa. Men with no shirts, or sleepy eyes, bed heads and sawdust still want their pictures taken with Santa.

It was not in grocery stores, however, that I learned the degree people don't care about their own appearance as long as the picture will be of them with Santa.

I learned on my first trip to a beauty shop filled with women on a Saturday morning many years ago. The women were in all stages of disarray. They were all ages from little girls to ladies with silver/blue hair. Still they wanted their picture with Santa, curlers, foil, rubber caps with hair pulled through, teased into a tribal "do", not withstanding. I could hardly believe it! Usually women squeal and hide when a man comes into their "parlor" to see them looking less than perfect, but not if he is Santa.

I go to a few beauty shops in memory of a dear friend who worked there. She loved God. She shampooed and curled Santa's beard and wig for years. She loved Santa. I always went to see her as Santa to give her a little recognition among her peers. Now that she has gone to spend her life with God, I go in remembrance of her and to help the ladies in the midst of toes, fingers and hair procedures feel the love of God.

Possibly my biggest revelation about pictures, however, came in hospitals, chemotherapy rooms, and dental clinics. People don't care if their hair is patchy or bald. They don't worry about tubes running into them from several sites. They don't care if their mouths are forced open with plastic dental appliances or if bloody gauze is showing. They don't mind if their cheeks are puffed out from other mysterious dental items. No one has worried about what they were wearing even if it was pajamas.

They just like having their picture made with Santa. When I am able, I get very close and hug them.

Sometimes I kneel by their bed or wheelchair. Sometimes I can only touch their shoulder and smile, but someone is there with a camera to take their picture.

It brings great joy to people of all ages, lifestyles, states of mind and body to have Santa stop, give a big smile and wait for their picture.

I feel like I am spreading God's love over and over again as those in the photo look at it over and over and show it to their friends and family. I can't always tell them that I wear the suit to tell people the story of Jesus and His birth at Christmas. I pray the message is there in the picture.

A Terrific Support Group

People driving by the hospital can see that this room is ready for a celebration of Christmas. The tree is tall and beautiful. The tables are set nicely and decorated. Boxes of the best stuffed animals I can find are already sitting around the tree and my chair is there waiting. Floor to ceiling windows make the decorations and celebration visible to any who drive past. The vision must lift their hearts.

My heart is already excited and happy and then I see the decorated vision before me complete now with groups of people near those tables and admiring the tree. I enter with expectation at seeing old friends from years past and a little dread because I know that some will be missing. This is a Brain Tumor Support group's Christmas party.

These people already know each other from meetings. I don't need to break the ice because they are friends. The patients have brought their families and everybody is in a holiday mood.

This is a grand affair. The food is gourmet catering. Who knew a hospital could produce such delicious fare? Although I cannot eat in the Santa suit, I know how good the food is because the catering staff packs me a huge dinner complete with dessert and puts it in my car. They get stuffed animals, too. Johnathan came to help me for many years and he still looks forward to the cheesecake "doggie boxes" I bring home.

The reason this is my favorite Christmas party and support group is not the food. These people exhibit such hope, joy, courage, perseverance and love for each other that it would be impossible not to admire them. Since families are together at the party, sometimes it is difficult to know which one is the patient. Sometimes the patient is obvious.

IF the patient is the father, the mother and children are struggling to deal with their new roles involving support money and comfort for the one who was their strength before the tumor. If the patient is the mother, everyone feels adrift taking on new roles at home and wanting to care perfectly for the one who cared for them. If the patient is a child, the whole family is disoriented trying to find time and resources to give him his every wish while maintaining medical schedules and the need for more money. Whoever is the patient, the illness seems hardest on the children.

I have been invited to this party for nearly 20 years. Many of the people and their families are just memories to us now. Many more are back showing their stubborn refusal to give up in spite of a terrible diagnosis. So many of the people know me that when I enter the room, they are truly excited to see me.

At some point in the festivities, they hand me a microphone and I am free to speak to the crowd. I have told them about God's candy cane heart. I greet them and try to give them encouragement as I see someone dressed up this year when they were in wheelchair before.

I congratulate them on bringing their families to the party. One year I told them that I could finally begin to understand what they were going through. I told them I had cancer and would be receiving treatment.

I tell them I pray for them and that year I asked them to pray for me. For several years they have let me pray a prayer of healing for the group and I do, praising God for all that He does, especially the miracles He works in people's lives.

When they come up to sit on my knee to receive their beautiful, soft animals, often they ask for me to pray individually for them. I always do, even when the lines are long.

My prayer is that God continues blessing these people with the best medical care in America, each patient with faith in Him, and me with the endurance and grace to continue this ministry to them.

Praying, Kneeling Santa

The first time I saw the figurine of the Santa Claus kneeling at the manger with baby Jesus, it was a gift from a teary friend. She said to me "When I saw this, I knew it was for you. This is what you represent in the lives of the people you cheer up at Christmas." That figure was one of the first in my collection of all things Santa. It still has a place of honor as the centerpiece among the painted starfish, music boxes, bungee jumping Santa things people have given me over the years. My collection includes a stuffed, custom Santa about 3 feet tall and his companion piece dressed in gold with a delicate porcelain face that we bought in Germany. This year a lady crocheted a long scarf of Santa's hat and face for me.

But the centerpiece is Santa at the manger, kneeling to worship the baby, Jesus. I pray that image will always be the centerpiece of my life and Santa ministry.

This Santa does pray with a lot of the people he sees. Some people want their prayers quiet and private. Many times I am able to include their visiting family and friends in the prayers. Several times I has been asked to pray for large groups. It became tradition at one Catholic elementary school for Santa to dismiss with prayer the entire school assembly for their Christmas holiday. At the end of that prayer, no one heard the "Amen" because the kids were racing for the doors.

 Santa stood a minute in silence, however, relishing the enormous opportunity God had given him to influence the little lives at that school.

Santa kneels many times a day during December. I thank God for a capable body as I have gotten older so that I can be close to people who are unable to get close to me on their own. I kneel by treatment chairs, bedsides, wheelchairs and easy chairs to be with people confined there. I kneel so that people can touch me, feel me touching them, hear me and be sure that I can hear their frail voices. With my face close to theirs, their family and friends have a good photo opportunity. I consider my kneeling with them as though I were kneeling to Jesus, kneeling with one of His "least of these" children that He loves.

Santa preaches! This Santa has been asked to preach from the pulpits of 4 denominations of churches in December. Sometimes the minister has chosen a topic for Santa to teach, but usually I preach my story of Jesus' birth, complete with oversized candy canes.

Some churches are quite formal with silk damask vestments and liturgy. Other churches are less formal with ministers in golf shirts and jeans. It doesn't matter to me because I wear the same suit. Usually the children have been allowed to stay for the sermon when I am preaching so I tailor the teaching to their level.

Some churches have a children's sermon which often becomes the main sermon when Santa is there to preach. This last Christmas the children were gathered together on the floor in front of the altar. I was standing in front of them and I asked, "What is the celebration we are waiting for that is coming soon?"

A cute little boy answered, "Christmas!"

I held an oversized candy cane (so it could be seen in the back of the church) upside down looking like the letter "J". "What does this look like?" I asked.

Another cute little boy answered knowingly, "A candy cane."

Fortunately God is there beside me to keep me from laughing out loud or floundering when the answer I seek does not come. I just smiled while the congregation roared until another child came up with the answer.

"Yes, and J stands for Jesus", I continued.

There were may pictures. Cute children knew the Christmas story and then it was time for Santa to leave. The Rector turned to me and said, "Santa, I thank you for coming to see us again this Christmas season.

I must say I am quite proud of our parish children for knowing their theology so well. I am especially relieved that my own son was able to remember that we were waiting eagerly to celebrate Christmas when you asked, because I was afraid he would say 'Star Wars' expected to be out in two weeks."

The story I tell is not a new story. It is the same story that has been told for more than 2000 years. My version of the story of Jesus' birth is not new either. I use candy canes to help people of all ages remember that together they form a heart. Whenever they see a candy cane for the rest of their lives, they can remember that heart and that God loves them. Jesus loves them, always.

"Glory to God in the highest and peace to his people on Earth."
The Book of Common Prayer

About the Author:

John Campbell, Santa Claus for 37 years, lives in Phoenix, Arizona with his wife, daughter and grandson. He still runs his advertising specialty business part time although he has not worked at all in December for more than 30 years.

He has never charged for a visit from Santa even though he has been to many private parties. Being Santa each December is a ministry for him. John has never received money or financial compensation for Santa work. He is a volunteer in the truest sense of the word. In recognition of his 25th year as Santa, he received an award from the President of the United States in appreciation of his services to the people of Arizona.

At first the cost of candy was the only expense. Then Santa saw the effect giving away stuffed animals had on the recipients and he wanted to give more. For a few years John and his family supported the purchase of bears and other gifts distributed to children and others who needed Santa's special touch entirely from their personal funds. Then the opportunity for expanded ministry and gifts came. Over the years many individuals and businesses have made contributions for the expenses of the Santa ministry. Most of the donors prefer to remain anonymous and their reward shall be in Heaven.

Santa John estimates that he has seen and touched over 320,000 people, not including congregations who have only been seen from afar, given out over 200,000 stuffed animals and 300,000 candy canes--one at a time.

John is president of North Pole Ministries, a 501(c)(3) tax exempt charity. North Pole ministries is also an Arizona Working Poor Qualifying Charity.

 Look for pictures that back up the stories in this book on the charity's website, www.NorthPoleMinistries.org.

Throughout the year, Santa John looks for people who need the kind of help North Pole ministries can provide. You may contribute to this ministry by going to the website located above. If you pay tax to Arizona a credit is available to you for your donation.

 You may email us at SantaMinistries@aol.com.

Supporting Scriptures for Santa John's Ministry

Matthew 18:10 "See that you do not despise one of these little ones, for I say to you, that their angels in Heaven continually behold the face of My Father who is in Heaven."

Mark 10:14 "Let the children come to me, do not hinder them; for to such belongs the kingdom of God."

Philippians 4:6 Be anxious for nothing, but in everything by prayer and supplication with thanksgiving let your requests be made known to God.

Philippians 2:3 Do nothing from selfishness or empty conceit, but with humility of mind let each of you regard one another as more important than himself.

Isaiah 49:26b And all flesh will know that I, the Lord, am your Savior and your Redeemer, the Mighty One of Jacob.

Matthew 25:40 And the King will answer them, "Truly I say to you, as you did it to one of the least of these my brethren, you did it to me."

I Peter 1:3-4 Blessed be the God and Father of our Lord Jesus Christ, who according to His great mercy has caused us to be born again to a living hope through the resurrection of Jesus Christ from the dead, to obtain an inheritance which is imperishable and undefiled and will not fade away, reserved in heaven for you.

John 3:17 For God did not send His Son into the world to judge the world, but that the world should be saved through Him.

Matthew 18:20 For where two or three have gathered together in My name, there I am in their midst.

Matthew 21:22 "And all things you ask in prayer, believing, you shall receive."

Matthew 23:39 "You shall love your neighbor as yourself."

Philippians 2:10 That at the name of Jesus, every knee should bow, of those who are in heaven, and on earth, and under the earth.

I Corinthians 13:13 And now abide faith, hope, love, these three; but the greatest of these is love.

Galatians 6:9 Let us never tire of doing good.

I Corinthians 15:58 Therefore, my beloved brethren, be steadfast, immovable, always abounding in the work of the Lord, knowing that your toil is not in vain in the Lord.

John 15:16-17 "You did not choose Me, but I chose you, and appointed you, that you should go and bear fruit, that whatever you ask of the Father in My name, He, may give to you. This I command you, that you love one another."

Colossians 3:2 Set your minds on things that are above, not on things that are on earth.

John 14:26 "Whatever you do in word or deed, do all in the name of the Lord Jesus, giving thanks."

John 14:27 "Peace I leave with you; My peace I give to you; not as the world gives do I give to you. Let not your hearts be troubled, neither let them be afraid.